BLACK FOUNDER

BLACK
FOUNDER

THE HIDDEN POWER
OF BEING AN OUTSIDER

STACY SPIKES

KENSINGTON PUBLISHING CORP.
www.kensingtonbooks.com

DAFINA BOOKS are published by

Kensington Publishing Corp.
119 West 40th Street
New York, NY 10018

PUBLISHER'S NOTE
This book is a memoir and as such, it consists of the author's recollections of the events, locations, and conversations recounted therein. In order to protect the privacy of some individuals, some names and identifying information have been changed.

All Kensington titles, imprints, and distributed lines are available at special quantity discounts for bulk purchases for sales promotion, premiums, fund-raising, educational, or institutional use. Special book excerpts or customized printings can also be created to fit specific needs. For details, write or phone the office of the Kensington Special Sales Manager: Attn. Special Sales Department, Kensington Publishing Corp, 119 West 40th Street, New York, NY 10018. Phone: 1-800-221-2647.

The DAFINA logo is a trademark of Kensington Publishing Corp.

ISBN: 978-1-4967-3956-8
First Kensington Hardcover Edition: February 2023

ISBN: 978-1-4967-3958-2 (e-book)

10 9 8 7 6 5 4 3 2 1

Printed in the United States of America

Library of Congress Control Number: 2022945640

To my wife and daughter,
you are my rock and my reason.

FALL DOWN SEVEN TIMES,
STAND UP EIGHT.

CONTENTS

BLACK FOUNDER

INTRODUCTION

I AM BLESSED TO be part of a community of founders who solve problems and look for ways to make things better in the world. Specifically, I help build technologies that connect storytellers and their audiences. Why do I do this? Because I have seen and personally experienced the transformative power of stories. The way they connect us. The way they help us through difficult times. They teach us lessons, and we develop different ways of thinking about things. We gain compassion and empathy for people we otherwise would not know.

The truly gratifying thing about being an entrepreneur is seeing a need and coming up with a way to fill it. And it's pretty cool to have an idea and be able to bring it to life.

If you are reading this, chances are you might be an entrepreneur too. You find yourself walking around in the world thinking, *Hey, I have an idea how to improve that.* You wake up in the middle of the night to scribble an idea in the notepad you keep on your nightstand to collect the thoughts that are always populating your mind. You might be starting your first business.

Maybe you are struggling to raise money. Maybe you've crashed and burned and have lost hope. Maybe you are feeling that familiar feeling that you don't have the right stuff. That you are not good enough. That you will be stuck at your desk job forever. That you're not cut out for this. That no one understands you and your ideas. That you are an outsider who doesn't fit in. Well, if any of that's true, you are in the right place.

Throughout my career and on many occasions, I have been all of these things. The outsider looking in on a world who didn't think I had what it would take to build a world-class product. I have met so many founders who've felt the same, especially women or founders of color. Being a founder is hard; it doesn't matter who you are. If you want to be a founder, it's not for the faint of heart. Being a member of this club means you will give everything you have to make something out of nothing, and if you get lucky, you might get a chance to share your experience to help those coming behind you. That is what I have attempted to do here with *Black Founder*.

In this book, I have related my personal experiences at different stages of my career. When I started out, I worked for others but felt that gnawing feeling that I was working so hard but I didn't own anything. Not only was I living paycheck to paycheck, I didn't even own my own work. Everything I did was in service to someone else. I was an instrument to fulfill their dreams. Finally, I took the leap to start my own business, crashing and burning several times before I was able to get traction. My trajectory had many ups and downs, but I believe there's a lot to be learned from someone's successes *and* failures. In fact, I would argue that the failures and challenges offer the greater lessons.

As I've said, throughout my life I've been viewed as an outsider, and that designation has often made my journey a little more difficult. However, being an outsider actually has many advantages. An outsider has a unique point of view and can see things others can't. Being an outsider, there are lower expectations of your being able to succeed, but being underestimated can make your entry a bit easier; no one is threatened by you because they don't even think you're in the game. Plus, the win is all the sweeter when they are taken by surprise. Being an outsider means you belong to a tribe of people who've faced similar obstacles, and they want to see you win. There are specific people and organizations that will want to help you raise capital, make connections, and gain access. Last but not least, being an outsider means you can be the first to do what no one else has done.

I don't want to downplay the challenges you will face. There are many. But you have the main ingredient you will need for success, and that is *you*! If you are going to be successful, it is going to be up to you and you alone. If you are going to be an entrepreneur, you must have a warrior mindset. Without it, you cannot make it. It doesn't matter if the odds are stacked against you and you think you have no way of winning. You need to move the ball forward.

Knowing you might lose and deciding to fight for your dreams anyway is liberating. Letting others know you will not quit is powerful and reaffirming. God helps those who help themselves. You have to be the answer to your questions, and you must believe in yourself.

I hope this book helps you reach your dreams. Today, success is too often measured in "unicorn status." The best measurement is in making something of quality that you are proud of because it helps others. Along your path don't forget to give back. When you have reached your version of success, write it down and pass it on so those behind you can stand on your shoulders, to make a difference as you did. When you see a founder doing great work and succeeding, congratulate them. More important, when you see a founder fall and perhaps have to close their doors, take a moment, write them a personal note, and ask if you can treat them to lunch. People did that for me, and I have to tell you it saved my life. This book is dedicated to them. *Black Founder* is not a book just for winners; it's a book for those who are willing to try!

—*Stacy Spikes*

CHAPTER 1

OUT THERE

I T WAS NEARING the end of my senior year of high school, and I did what many kids do: I decided to follow my dream. And my dream was to move to Hollywood. I didn't have a fully baked plan, but music and films were calling me. This idea seems absolutely crazy now. What is it about youth that makes us so bold and fearless? All I know is that my hometown felt too small. I needed to chase my dreams. I was losing the siren call to that confident kid in my bedroom mirror at home. I was eighteen years old and working at Sound Warehouse off the Katy Freeway in Houston, Texas. Sound Warehouse was where my love of movies and music collided. I spent most of my days after school working in the video section of the store, renting movies to customers and restocking the returns to the shelves while songs from the latest album releases played in the background. I loved working there but knew there was no future for me. It seemed everyone who worked at the store had the same deep understanding that if we didn't leave as soon as we could, we would all get married, have kids, and die there.

My parents were aware of my restless heart. They both graduated from Grambling State University, a historically Black college in Louisiana known for its amazing football program and world-famous marching band. My parents met there, and it was their hope that my brother and I would also graduate from Grambling. I didn't completely reject this idea, but I needed to see if I could make my dreams happen first. Being from a proud Black family with parents who were a part of their families' first generation to go to college, I felt their expectations and the expectations of my ancestors on my shoulders. I struggled with how to broach the subject of moving to California with my parents.

I spoke to my high school career counselor, Ms. Fry. She was very kind and understood my conflict, and she gave me advice that changed the trajectory of my life. She told me that I had to live a life that I would not regret.

I was not sure how my parents were going to respond. My mother modeled the concept of following your dreams. She owned her own business with her name on the door, and she was always talking about new ideas. She even had her own public access television show. My father was very creative. He was a school principal and very serious about our grades, but he was also a talented artist. He was self-taught and could do incredible pencil drawings. On the weekends, my dad had a booth where he sold his art. He was so proud when he sold one of his drawings. Both of them were very hardworking people who often had two or three jobs each to make sure we had a roof over our heads and a comfortable life. I can remember many hot Texas summers when my dad worked for Sears installing carpet to supplement his teacher's salary. They did not want my brother and me to struggle the way they did, and, in their minds, education was key.

I mustered up the courage to talk to my parents and let them know my plan. I started with the easier one, my mom. She was supportive and told me to go follow my dreams. Two of her brothers lived in the Los Angeles area, and I think she figured they could keep an eye on me. I suspect she also thought this was just a phase, that I would go out to LA and quickly realize that I was chasing empty dreams and that California wasn't all it was cracked up to be. Then there was my father. He was going to be a bit more of a challenge. As a school principal, my dad was all about education. Think of Morgan Freeman as Principal Joe Clark in *Lean on Me* and you would have a pretty accurate picture of my father. He was all business and did not suffer fools gladly. And according to him, anyone who didn't pursue an education was a fool.

I was absolutely terrified. I could hear my heart beating in my ears. I made my voice as deep as I could, puffed out my chest, and walked up to my dad—who was in the kitchen making dinner—and dropped the hammer.

"Dad, I've made a decision: I'm moving to California to follow my dreams."

"Oh really?" my father asked. (As a parent myself now, I have come to realize this was more a question of my sanity than anything else.) "How much money do you have?"

Proudly I told him, "Three hundred dollars."

He just raised his eyebrow in response. I hurriedly added that I would be taking only a year off and then would go to college. That wasn't really my plan, but I was confident that I would be so successful before the year was out that he could have no objections to my decision. I braced myself for his rebuttal (or his outrage), but he just sighed deeply, shaking his head. It wasn't a resounding yes, but it also wasn't a no. I'm sure he figured I would be calling to come home by the time I hit Albuquerque.

I had a little pickup truck, and I made my way to my uncle Joe's house. He and his family actually lived in Orange County. I didn't realize how far it was from LA, but it was okay because I had a nothing-is-going-to-stop-me attitude, and I was excited for what lay ahead. The drive from Texas to California seemed to fly by, the exhilarating feeling of freedom fueling me. I only stopped twice on the way, but by the time I arrived at my uncle's house, it was pretty late and I was exhausted. I parked on the street and knew I couldn't leave all my stuff in the flatbed, but I didn't want to wake up the whole house taking it inside. Not that I had much; I had packed my things into three large black trash bags to prevent my belongings from getting wet on my drive. I decided I would just drag the bags into the garage and sort them in the morning. When I had called my uncle earlier, he told me he would leave a key in the mailbox for me, and I should just head to the den and get some sleep, so I let myself in and passed out on the couch that my aunt had set up for me.

When I woke up the next morning, I heard the clatter of dishes and smelled breakfast and brewing coffee. My aunt and cousins greeted me warmly and quickly made me a plate.

As I was eating, I saw my uncle coming in from the garage and said to him, "I'll move those bags in just a bit."

"Which bags?"

I said, "Those heavy black trash bags."

He laughed and said, "I thought those were trash. What's in them?"

"Everything!"

I ran outside to see the garbage truck making the turn at the end of the street. I ran after it screaming, but it didn't stop. All my belongings were gone. When I walked back into the house, I could tell everyone was trying hard not to laugh.

My uncle said, "Hey, a word of advice . . . Don't put your things in trash bags. People might think they're trash."

The family got a kick out of that and burst out laughing. Things were off to a great start.

———

ORANGE COUNTY WAS in a housing boom, and I was able to get work doing day labor building houses. I mostly moved lumber. I saved everything I made until I had enough money to move into an apartment in Sherman Oaks with a roommate named Todd. Todd had two or three jobs at any given time, and we rarely saw each other. I soon realized you needed more than one job to get by in this city, and, in short order, I had three jobs. By day, I worked as a gopher at a video sales company. By night, I loaded trucks for UPS. On weekends, I did concert security. And in my spare time, I worked on my music. I was busy hustling, but it was good, clean living and I was young. My parents were proud to see me working hard and making my way in the world. They even came out to visit and made sure I was living right.

Unfortunately, I got injured working at the UPS job. I pulled a muscle lifting a very small but deceptively heavy box and was put on medical leave. And that was all it took to get me introduced to an entirely new set of friends and SoCal nightlife. Let's just say I fell in with some very bad characters and was doing things that I was not writing home about. It was the San Fernando Valley in 1987. The crowd I ran with was filled with foolish bravado and took me places I had never seen. I couldn't believe how far and how fast I had fallen. I was afraid of who I had become.

My family began to worry. I wasn't calling home anymore. My grandmother called one day and left a message saying that they had been praying for me at her church and she had been saying her rosary over me.

I hated that my family was worried. I decided to invite my uncle Joe and his family over to show them I was doing okay. My apartment building had a nice pool with picnic tables and barbecue grills. We'd have a cookout, and the kids could play in the pool. I knew this would be a great opportunity to calm my family down and let them know I had everything under control. I was actually excited to have them come over. Early the morning of the cookout, I went out for groceries and got everything ready. I told myself I was not going to touch anything that day. I was going to show them I got this.

I told Uncle Joe to arrive at noon. By eleven I was getting antsy. I wanted everything to be perfect; I didn't want to mess anything up. I thought I would do a little something to help take the edge off. I didn't want to have the monkey on my back with the kids around. A voice in my head told me that was a bad idea, but I did it anyway. I started to relax; I felt good. So good that I must have dozed off. The intercom buzzer startled me. They had arrived. I told them to go straight back to the pool, that I just needed to grab some things and I would be right there. I never made it. I never saw them.

I came to the next day. There was a note under my door. *We hope you're okay. We don't know what happened to you.* My answering machine was blinking. The machine was full. The first messages were from my uncle. Then my mother called. Three times. The voices on the messages were concerned, then angry and fed up.

I was so sick I felt like I was going to die, but I knew I needed to face the music. I called my mother and braced myself. But she didn't scream and holler.

In a calm voice she just said, "Son, I think you have a problem, just like my father did when he returned from WWII. I am afraid for you, but I won't sit around and watch you kill yourself just like he did. It breaks my heart, but I have accepted your death," and she hung up.

The room was spinning, and it felt like an elephant was sitting on my chest. I dropped the phone and realized I couldn't feel the fingers on my right hand. I felt like I was freezing. At that moment, my roommate, Todd, walked through the door.

He said, "Man, you look awful. Are you okay?"

I shook my head, not able to make eye contact. I felt both scared and ashamed. He asked if I needed help, and I just nodded. Then he asked if I would like him to take me to the hospital, and I nodded again.

It was a hot October day, and Todd had the windows of his red Camaro down, but I was so cold. I felt like I had the flu. Maybe that was it. Maybe I was just sick.

I really don't remember them checking me into the hospital. The first couple of days were a blur. By the third day, I was ready to go. The doctors had talked to me, but I was sure it was all a mistake. They were overreacting. They said I had a mild heart attack, but that was impossible. I just needed to get out of there. I let the nurses know that I was feeling much better and that I would be going home soon. I had to get back to my job. My bosses at the video company were going to fire me. I'd already missed two days of work, and they had no idea where I was. The nurses allowed me to call my boss, William. He was a good guy and he liked me, but I knew he was going to be angry. I explained what was going on and assured him I would be at work the next day.

"You'll do no such thing," William hollered. "If you leave the hospital before the doctors say you should, you won't have a job to come back to!"

What? Was he conspiring with the hospital? I didn't need this place. I just had a bad weekend.

They transferred me to another floor and said I had to take part in some program. It felt like a prison. I had to sit in these meetings, and speakers would come in and talk. Well, I wasn't interested, and I didn't believe a word they were saying. And I wasn't shy about letting them know how unhappy I was to be there. One of the other "inmates" told me to shut up, that I was disturbing the meeting, before stomping off. Yeah, whatever. Before I knew it, the snitch returned with Nurse Barbara. Think Nurse Ratched from *One Flew Over the Cuckoo's Nest*.

Nurse Barbara said, "Mr. Spikes, can I see you in my office?"

I glared at the snitch as I left the room. Nurse Barbara told me to sit down. Her office was small and cramped, but well organized.

She was silent for a few minutes, just looking at me, and then said, "You don't seem to want to be here, Mr. Spikes. These hospital beds are hard to come by. You are here because you have insurance to pay for this, but there is a waiting list for these beds. What we don't tolerate is anyone preventing others from getting the recovery they need, and, Mr. Spikes, you are robbing others of that opportunity. I have warned you before, and this was the last time. I want you out of my hospital."

I couldn't agree with her more. I wanted out too. She stood up and opened her office door. Just as I was about to walk out, she stopped me and said, "There's one more thing that I want to tell you. You are young and you could have your whole life ahead of you, but you're going to walk out of here and end up coming back in a body bag. I don't feel sorry for you; I feel sorry for anyone who loves and cares about you because you are going to break their heart, and it's such a waste. Now get out of my hospital."

I walked out of her office, and she slammed the door behind me.

Shaken, I went back to my room and began packing my things. Nurse Barbara had scared me, and I could believe that perhaps my life was in more danger than I knew. I heard my grandmother's voice saying she was praying for me. I heard my mother acknowledging my death. I knew I had caused my family so much pain. The reality of my impact on others came crashing in. I began to weep, crying ugly tears. I had been so selfish, just thinking about having fun, but I had put my life in danger so many times, never thinking of the consequences.

Just at that moment, I heard a loud commotion outside my room. I heard a door bang open and voices shouting commands. I peeked out and saw a gurney being rushed down the hall. A man was sitting on top of a girl, pumping her chest while doctors and paramedics ran alongside. They wheeled the gurney into a room. I remember seeing the bottom of the girl's feet, blackened with dirt, clearly from walking without shoes.

The door closed and people were walking frantically in and out of the room. Then I heard one of the paramedics talking to a nurse just outside my door. The girl was a heroin addict who OD'd. They had been able to revive her but didn't think she would make it through the night. The staff knew her; she had been there before.

I went back into my room and sat quietly on the edge of my bed, knowing there was a young woman fighting for her life just down the hall. And somehow, thinking about that girl and my grandfather—my mother's father—who I never met, I knew that if I walked out of that hospital that day, there was a good chance I would fulfill Nurse Barbara's prophecy.

I slid down on the side of my bed and got on my knees. My prayer was simple: *Please God, help me and I swear I will never drink or take drugs ever again. I will do whatever it takes. Don't let me die.*

I was nineteen years old, and with God's help, I have not had a drink or a drug since.

CHAPTER 2

ALL THAT GLITTERS

THROUGHOUT MY JOURNEY, I have had countless guides I have met along the way—guides who have introduced me to the world, showed me what traps to avoid, and helped light the way. You will get to meet many of them in these pages. I found such a person at my first real job in Los Angeles, where I returned when I got out of the hospital. I worked at a company called Powersports American Video in Encino, which was actually made up of two different companies. Powersports licensed ESPN racing such as Formula 1, motocross, off-road racing, and more. There was a strong cult following for these titles. We would repackage the races, cutting them with music and exciting edits. At the end of the year, we would do a compilation of all the crashes called the Havoc series. These titles were big with the late-night direct-response market. Did you ever watch late-night television and see one of those As Seen on TV commercials? It might have been for a high-speed blender or something. The announcer quotes a super low price, like $19.99, and says, "But wait, there's more!" Then they would throw in a bunch of other items, and then again say, "But wait, there's more! If you call within the next thirty minutes, we'll throw in a free set of knives!" A 1-800 number would flash across the screen and the words *Call now! Limited time offer!* would pulsate. That's direct-response marketing. So imagine that with racing videos and heavy metal music.

American Video, the other division, licensed low-budget titles from the studios and packaged them as space-filler titles in your favorite video store. We worked out of a three-bedroom house just off Ventura Boulevard. The company was owned by two Israeli Jews—William, the CEO, and his business partner, Joe. The total staff was about seven people. What was amazing about working for them was that for a large part of the day, I would just hear Hebrew. I knew a little bit of Spanish growing up in Texas, but Hebrew was something else. I loved the language. I was around the same age as William's sons, who would come and work in the office sometimes after school and during the summer. William's wife, Mickey, treated me like I was her own child. She would say, "Stacy, we are going to send you to Israel to live on a kibbutz and you're going to meet a nice Jewish girl." And I really did feel like part of the family. If it wasn't for William and Joe threatening the loss of my job, I would have never stayed in rehab, and I don't think it's an exaggeration to say they probably saved my life.

The job itself was exciting at times, and I learned a lot of skills that serve me to this day. And working there was entertaining. Joe and William were crazy negotiators. These guys fought over every penny. I remember Joe on the phone having a screaming match with someone on the other end of the line. He would yell, "You're trying to rob me! Do I look like an idiot? You must think I'm stupid! This invoice says five thousand dollars! I thought we were friends. If this is how you treat your friends, then how do you treat your enemies?" On and on the battle would go. Every now and then he'd hang up, slamming the phone receiver down, and then continue arguing with the phone even though no one was there. The vendor would call back, and there'd be more yelling. Then all of a sudden, a price would be reached and there was peace. There was laughter, and then they'd ask, "When are we having dinner?" It was better than watching wrestling! I can't say I ever became such a great negotiator, but William and Joe introduced the idea that every-thing was negotiable so you might as well try.

Working there, my Hebrew got pretty good. I knew some basic phrases and how to count. They taught me a few bad words too. At some point, I realized I wasn't making enough money and I needed to ask for a raise. I knew this could be bad. I was terrified to go to William and ask him. How do I negotiate a raise with a master negotiator who didn't want to pay an extra dime? Some of my friends at the company told me I should go ask for my raise in Hebrew. I thought it was a risky strategy, but I was willing to try anything. With a little bit of tutoring from my coworkers, I was ready to go to William and make my request. I stood outside his office until Donna, William's assis-tant, gave me the sign he was off his call. I went to the open door and knocked, standing at the threshold.

"What? I'm busy," he grunted, not looking up from his desk.

I walked into his office and stood behind one of the guest chairs. I cleared my throat and, as authoritatively as I could in my fledgling Hebrew, I said, "William, I want a raise." William stared at me for a moment, then burst out laughing, saying, "You're becoming a Jew. Now get out of my office."

I walked out the door and yelled back, "Do I get my raise?"

"Go away!" he responded.

I got my raise.

Did I get the raise because I asked in Hebrew? Perhaps. I believe William knew I was a hard worker and probably deserved the raise. But what I did learn about negotiating was sometimes you can come from a different direction. It means a lot to someone that you are willing to go to extra lengths to meet them on their field. Think outside the box and relate with them. See the world through their eyes.

———

IN THE OFFICE there was this character, Lou Drozen. To me, Lou was a cantankerous old man who looked like a Vegas boss right out of *Casino*. As far as I could tell, Lou was well-known and respected in the business and acted as a "rabbi" who helped William and Joe navigate the crazy entertainment industry. Lou was the founder of Laff Records, one of the first record labels for comedians like Redd Foxx, Richard Pryor, LaWanda Page, and Leroy & Skillet—Black comics of the day whose off-color jokes about sex, race, and Black life were groundbreaking. Laff Records was also one of the first record companies releasing comedy records called party records. Party records had a dual meaning. Often, they were recorded at a small party in someone's home or in a bar where a comedian would tell jokes in front of a live audience. You can see scenes of this in Eddie Murphy's movie *Dolemite Is My Name*. These records became known as party records because people would have a party and put these records on in the background.

When I was growing up, my parents had a large mahogany cabinet record player in the living room. It was a heavy piece of furniture, and I loved the deep brown color and the rich smell of the wood. To me, it was a magic machine. The piston hinges glided the top up to reveal the record player on the left and the radio on the right. Two large speakers were encased in the front of the cabinet. One of the good things about the system is that you could plug in headphones. This stereo had the most astounding effect on my life. This record player was my entry into the world beyond my street, my city, and everything I knew. All my allowance money and any money I made mowing lawns went toward purchasing twelve-inch vinyl albums. I bought albums from Pink Floyd; Parliament Funkadelic; Earth, Wind & Fire; Prince; Rush; the Isley Brothers; the Smiths; Iron Maiden; Van Halen; and so much more. I learned to play guitar at that machine, lifting its needle over and over until I got a riff or arrangement right. At the time, I thought nothing in the world had the power this machine had. In my opinion, the record player was superior to the radio because I controlled the experience. I was the DJ. There were no commercial breaks, and I could listen to the same track or album all day or all month if I wanted to. My personal radio station had no limits and needed no sponsors. It was just for me, by me, and I controlled the playlist.

I was always playing in my parents' closet, as kids are wont to do. My dad had these very cool platform shoes I used to like to wear and strut around in when they weren't home. One day I found there was a secret stash of records buried deep in the corner. I knew they must've been special if they were hidden in the very back of my parents' closet. Some of the records were even in paper bags. *Huh, this must be good*, I thought. Redd Foxx, Richard Pryor, Laff Records. What could be on those records that would make my parents hide them away? I put one of the albums under my shirt and ran to my bedroom. I shoved the record under my bed, determined to resolve the mystery. That night, when the house was quiet and asleep, I snuck into the living room, plugged my headphones into the record player, and put on the record. I never laughed so hard in my life. I had to cover my mouth with a pillow so I wouldn't wake anyone up and get busted. After that night, I would regularly sneak one of those albums out of my parents' closet and go to the living room after everyone was asleep to listen. I eventually got caught listening to Richard Pryor; I guess I was just laughing too loud.

So, before there were Kevin Hart, Chris Rock, or Wanda Sykes there were Redd Foxx and Richard Pryor. And there I was sitting with the man who helped introduce these geniuses to the world, listening to his stories about how it all began. It was mind-blowing, to say the least. In Black culture, messages could be hidden between the beats of a song. The music of Bob Marley, James Brown, or Billie Holiday was rebellious. For a young Black boy, these songs did something. But Black comedy albums were something else! Redd Foxx or Richard Pryor would just come out and say things, sometimes right to a white audience, things that could get you killed. I had never seen courage like that. They didn't hide behind a 4/4 beat; they said what they wanted to say right to your face. They talked about racism and its harsh brutality all while making you laugh.

In Lou's office were boxes of original masters of some of the most influential comedians ever recorded. I felt like a kid in a candy store. I'd sit in Lou's office after everyone had gone home, and he would tell me countless stories about how these comedians fought for civil rights and broke down barriers in their own unique way. I wish Lou had written a book. He was a walking historian, and I was one of the luckiest kids in the world to hear his stories firsthand.

Lou was a good guy, and he treated me well. He'd always pull this huge wad of money from his pocket and peel off a couple of twenties, telling me to grab him a sandwich, get whatever I wanted, and keep the change. On good days, I'd come back to Lou's office and we'd eat our sandwiches listening to one of the masters of Redd Foxx or Richard Pryor, with Lou pausing the tape to tell me the backstory of the scene and craziness that went into that particular recording. It was priceless.

Around this time, Black cinema was exploding, thanks in large part to Spike Lee. I grew up watching videos of old films from the seventies like *Shaft*, *Superfly*, *Foxy Brown*, *Dolemite*, *Sweet Sweetback's Baadasssss Song*, and *Cotton Comes to Harlem*. But a renaissance was happening now, and I wanted to be part of it. Denzel Washington was a huge influence on so many, including me. This brother was smart. He wasn't just playing thug roles. His on-screen characters deeply influenced the man I wanted to be in life. Movies like *A Soldier's Story* and *Cry Freedom* showed that our stories had depth, weight, and range.

Denzel was my generation's Sidney Poitier and Harry Belafonte all rolled into one.

Because of him I started taking acting classes. I liked them quite a bit and found them almost therapeutic. Acting always felt like a return to innocence, like when you are young and playing make-believe with your friends. But acting was more than pretend play. A good performance could bring a character to life, create a parallel reality, and elicit strong, genuine emotions. Acting takes talent, sure. But there are also skills that a performer must learn to master. I found that some aspects of acting were harder than others. Anger came easily, but being funny was a lot more difficult than I thought it would be. Making humor seem spontaneous is very challenging. I learned a lot and saw that acting is a craft that requires talent, hard work, and dedication. Those classes gave me an added level of respect for actors I have always admired. To this day, when I am watching a movie, I wonder if I could perform a particular scene. How would I approach it? How would I be able to make those feelings well up inside me? And that just makes me love movies even more—because I know all the hard work that goes into them.

My acting teacher said the only way we learn is by doing and insisted that we go out there and audition. It wasn't enough to learn the craft of acting; we needed to learn the business of acting. We had to go on casting calls and come back each week and talk about our experiences. I went on many casting calls—some for larger films, some for student or independent films, and some for commercials. If there were any casting calls for a young Black male, I was there.

Every audition seemed to be the same: a group of Black men out in the lobby, and when you got into the room, a table full of white faces. The process went like this: When you arrive, you check in and they give you a page or two of a scene. You do the best you can to digest the lines and make this character come alive in time to walk in front of the firing squad and persuade them to hire you.

Rap music was influencing our culture, and movies like *Boyz n the Hood* and *New Jack City* had just come out. So it was no surprise that most of the casting calls were for Black thugs. I knew that no matter how you dressed me up, I didn't make an impressive thug. Geek, yes; thug, definitely not. But I didn't want to go back to class empty-handed, so I got out there and went for those roles.

There's one memorable audition that epitomizes most of the casting calls I went on. I arrived and checked in. I looked around and saw a lot of brothers in white muscle shirts who clearly spent more time in the gym than I ever did. I was deeply intimidated. I was much smaller, didn't have any tattoos, and I'm sure I was the only guy there in a Ralph Lauren polo shirt. I was handed my lines and a description of the scene: Some white college kids were out camping in a desert location and sitting around a campfire. The thug (my character) was to ambush them, rob them, and take one of the girls and their car.

I started pacing around, trying to memorize my lines, and then I heard my name called. I was directed to a room down the hall, walked in, and shut the door behind me. The casting team had my headshot, and we did general introductions. Behind the table sat three white guys and one white girl, all in their twenties, like me.

The casting director smiled and said, "Okay, whenever you're ready."

I don't remember the exact lines, and I've omitted the unnecessary profanity, but the scene went something like this:

THUG walks up behind the kids sitting around the campfire with their backs to him.

THUG: First person that moves gets shot.

WHITE BOY 1:   What the hell are you doing?

THUG: Shut up and sit down!

Thug pistol-whips him.

THUG: Anybody else want some of this?

No one moves or says anything.

THUG: I didn't think so.

"Stop!" the director yelled from behind the table. "I need more street, more thug. You are from the toughest projects. And don't hold your gun like that. Hold it like a real thug—you know, up in the air turned sideways, pointing down."

He stood up to demonstrate, grabbing his crotch in his "thug stance," arm in the air, pointing his thumb and forefinger as if he's holding a gun. Then he sat down and barked, "Go again!"

I read my lines again, this time in the most stereotypical thug voice I could muster. I sounded ridiculous. The group at the table whispered to one another, nodding. They said thanks and called for the next thug to come in. I remember I got in my truck and felt so dirty and had this feeling of disgust for even reading those lines. Sitting there, parked right across the street from the audition space, I watched other Black actors, in their baggy pants and muscle tees, practicing lines on the front lawn. It made my stomach turn. It wasn't that I believed we shouldn't play some of the stereotypes of Black culture but more a feeling of *Is this all there is?* Way back then I knew I wanted to change this game. I didn't like what I saw or how I felt, and this was not okay with me. As these emotions swirled around inside me, I tried to separate the feelings of rejection, humiliation, racism, classism. I asked myself if I would have felt differently if I were auditioning for Spike Lee. I thought if Black people were making a movie with thugs or gangsters, it would have more depth and dimension. We should be telling our own stories.

Think about Delroy Lindo's character in Spike Lee's *Malcolm X*. Lindo plays West Indian Archie, who is a mobster who runs the streets and takes young Malcolm under his wing. Archie is a complex character with depth. He had an amazing ability to memorize long sequences of numbers, never having to write them down. However, due to life circumstances, he used his gift for criminal activities. He was not your stereotypical mobster, and Delroy Lindo, portraying Archie, wasn't directed to act like a thug. In the hands of a Black director, you will get richer character development, not a cardboard cutout. That to me was the difference.

I remember seeing *Devil in a Blue Dress*, based on the Walter Mosely novel and directed by Carl Franklin. In it, Denzel plays Easy Rawlins, a private detective hired to find a missing woman. That character is interesting, well-rounded; he has substance.

Commercials weren't any better. I remember going on a casting call for a commercial for a national burger chain. When

I arrived, there was a waiting room full of Black men and women of all ages. The audition sheet had one line on it: "Mmmmm, that burger sho is good." I read it and thought to myself, *Who speaks like this?* The auditions were quick. An actor would go in, come out two minutes later, and the next would go in. This was a fast-paced assembly line. I could hear the muffled sounds of the others as they went into the audition room and was able to adapt my line based on the feedback they were getting.

It was finally my turn. After the usual introductions, they instructed me to look at the camera and say the line. Since the line was so short and you didn't need to memorize it, they wanted me to act as if I had an actual burger in my hands, take a bite, and say the line.

"Go whenever you're ready," said the casting director.

I pretended I had a burger in my hands, took a bite, and said, "Mmmmm, that burger sure is good."

The white director said, "Okay . . . that was great, but can you try again? The phrasing that we are looking for is 'sho is good.' Okay, got it? Now try again."

My second attempt came out as "show is good." The casting director asked if I would like to give it one more shot, and on my third try I made my best attempt at Ebonics, saying the line perfectly. But everyone in the room knew it was not convincing. They thanked me, and I left. That was the last time I ever went on an audition for a movie or a commercial.

By day, I listened to Lou telling stories about brave Black comedians telling white people where they could go, and at these auditions I just felt like a coward. I know some people followed this path and did parts they felt were beneath them to get their foot in the door, but I just couldn't stomach it. I believed there had to be a better way for me.

CHAPTER 3

MENTORS OF MOTOWN

W ORKING AT POWERSPORTS American Video was amazing because it was such a small company and I was able to learn all about the business, how everything worked from end to end. This was the classic apprentice style of learning, where you get to experience and learn a trade firsthand. I started out at American as a gopher, but before long I was working with the art directors on the box designs. This was before everything was digital, so the process was a bit more involved, but this is how it worked: We would get the masters of a film that we had purchased the rights to. I would rent out a screening room and watch the film, noting the time code of images that might work for the video box. Then I had to take the master to a video transfer house, give them the time codes, and they would give me the images. From there, the images and the general concept would go to a freelance art director who would first give us some sketches of video box concepts. Once we chose a direction, the art director would give us three different looks based on the concept from the images pulled from the movie. And once we settled on a cover, the art director would put together a proof to be sent to the printer.

We worked with a company called Modern Album. They were one of the biggest printers of album jackets at the time but were moving into printing video boxes. Once we signed off on the proofs, Modern Album would make the four-color printing plates: cyan, magenta, yellow, and black. Each color was laid one at a time as it ran through the press, so at times you had to add more of a specific color ink to get the colors right. Part of my job was to be on-site at the printer to ensure that the box colors got as close as possible to our proof. I loved this part of the process. I felt so powerful when a sheet would come off the line and it was put on the production table. The floor supervisor would bend over the table and look at it through a loupe. They would weigh in and tell you if the red was too high or the black too low. I always tended to agree, but it was cool that that final call was mine.

Through Lou, I got to know the Pine family, who owned Modern Album, and I became friendly with Josh Pine, the son of the owner. While waiting for the printing jobs, I would hang out with him and talk about music and the industry. I loved the mechanical, rhythmic sound of the printing presses and the sweet smell of the inks.

One day while I was at Modern Album, I overheard one of the sales reps from another company mention that Berry Gordy had sold Motown to Universal Music and the company was moving to LA and hiring. The rep must have noticed me listening because she turned to me and said that if I was interested in the job, she could put in a good word with Stephen Meltzer, the creative director, who she was friends with.

"Just have your book ready to show them," she said.

Book? I didn't have a book. I didn't even know what a book was. But I gave her my card, and she said she would pass it along to Stephen.

I was excited about the opportunity to interview for Motown, but I wasn't sure I wanted to work at a record label. I wanted to be *signed by* a record label. I still considered myself an artist and was starting to make some inroads with my music career. And I had invested a lot—time and money—into my music. I had a full MIDI recording studio in my bedroom that consisted of a KORG M1 synthesizer, TASCAM drum machine, mixing board, 8-track recorder, mics, and two guitars. I was deeply committed to my music and believed that was my destiny. I thought if I worked at a label, I would lose my edge and become a suit. In my mind, that would be the worst thing that could happen.

Well, sometimes fate intervenes in your life and completely changes your plans. Between the time that the rep offered to make the introduction to the creative director at Motown and the time I had my meeting with Stephen, something happened that made me wonder if the universe was trying to direct my steps. I came home from work one evening and found that my apartment had been robbed. The nation was in the grips of a cocaine epidemic, and addicts were desperate, doing whatever was needed to get high. The police said there was a string of robberies in the area, and I guess now it was my turn. Everything was gone, and I was completely devastated. How could this happen to me? It had taken me years to acquire all that equipment, and I lost it all. My apartment was on the ground floor in the back of the building, near the parking lot. The police said whoever committed the crime probably knew me and knew when and where to strike. This hardened my soul. The bloom started to fade off the rose of my LA dreams. That mystery of the robbery was never solved, but it proved to be one of those little twists of fate that changed my life forever. I've since realized that sometimes the worst things that happen to you are the best things. As hard as setbacks are, you must keep your head up and walk through these times. They build your character and make you who you are. You have to be strong and faithful. Don't let them break you. Let them make you.

So, having to replace all my music equipment made the job at Motown much more attractive. I knew the pay would be more than I was currently making, and I needed all the cash I could get so I could rebuild my home system as quickly as possible. Someone mentioned to me that Marvin Gaye answered phones at Motown before he got his recording contract. I don't know if that is true, but I chose to believe it. Now I just needed to figure out what a "book" was. I asked around, and a friend who was a photographer told me it was a portfolio, and I needed to put one together that contained some of the video boxes I worked on.

When I first met Stephen Meltzer, my initial thought was that he was really cool and sophisticated. He was a tall, slender white man with salt-and-pepper hair and a simple, neat look. His office was like nothing I had ever seen. It was a minimalist design. When you stood in the doorway of his office, you felt like you were about to enter a peaceful sanctuary. The overhead lights were off, and the tall window shades were down. You couldn't tell if it was night or day. Instead of a desk in the middle of the room, there was a table against one wall. A sleek lamp sat on top of it, casting a warm glow in the corner of the room. The whole vibe was peaceful and inviting.

Steven ushered me to a chair and then sat across from me. He thanked me for coming, and we chatted for a minute before he reached out to look at my portfolio, which I had slaved over and was very nervous to show him. He had these beautiful black-and-white photos of Motown artists on the walls of his office, and I felt like just opening my portfolio would release four-color chaos in this museum-like office.

Stephen went through my portfolio without comment, and only when he closed it did he say, "I love your work. You're very talented." He said he wanted me to meet with the head of the creative department, a man named Jonathan Clark. He stepped out of his office for a moment, and when he returned he said that Jonathan would be in shortly. He also warned me that Jonathan could be high energy but that I shouldn't be put off by that.

After a few minutes, Jonathan burst into the room. A tall, wiry ball of energy who reminded me of Samuel Jackson, Jonathan was all street: sneakers, jeans, basketball jersey, baseball cap turned backward, and cigarette in his mouth. Some people hold their cigarette between their first two fingers. Jonathan would come in sideways across his face and down on the cigarette, pinching it between his forefinger and thumb from above after a drag. Jonathan was like that bad uncle who was cool and you kind of wanted to be like but deep down knew that was a bad idea. He moved as if he were made of sound, like an animated character from the Spider-Verse. He walked up to me and shook my hand vigorously, pumping his arm up and down almost like striking a drum. After the introductions, he turned to Stephen and said, "Damn! What are you? A vampire? Man, it's dark in here. . . . Hold on!" And with that, he walked out of the room.

We could hear him cursing and complaining about something outside in the hall. Stephen and I just sat there waiting, but then Stephen rose and motioned for me to follow him.

When Jonathan saw us approaching, he barked, "Stephen, when does he start?"

Stephen turned and looked at me over the top of his glasses, waiting for an answer.

"Two weeks?" I suggested.

Jonathan nodded and walked away.

"I guess I'll see you in two weeks," said Stephen.

I didn't even really know what the job was, but I assumed I'd be a gopher in the art department. It was hard to leave Lou, William, and the whole American Video family, but there were new adventures ahead, and they wished me well and thought it was a good opportunity.

————

WORKING AT MOTOWN was the first time I ever worked at an all-Black company. It wasn't that *everyone* was Black, but it was the opposite of the world I had worked in before. The CEO was Black, as well as 90 percent of the staff. I heard that when Berry Gordy sold Motown to Universal (MCA) he made a stipulation that Motown had to always have a Black CEO. This was amazing to me. Motown was a cultural institution, and to stipulate that the CEO needed to be Black meant there was a commitment to ensure that its cultural integrity remained intact.

My primary job was to get album art approved. Album art had to route to each of the main department heads for their comments before it finally got to the CEO, Jheryl Busby. The artist also had to sign off on the art. Depending on the comments, the comps would get changed and updated as they made their way to final approval. And it was my responsibility to make sure the art was seen by everyone who needed to see it. I felt like I had the most important job at the company.

What was great about this job is that I got to meet and know all the department heads—A&R (artists and repertoire, the department that scouts new talent and oversees the artistic development of the artists), marketing, sales, public relations, international sales, video, promotion, finance, legal—and the COO and CEO. While this was happening inside the company, I had to also help coordinate getting the album art approved by the artist. For the most part, this was done through A&R reps, since they usually had the best relationship with the artists. A&R were the cool kids in the company. They would stroll into the office sometime after 10:00 a.m. but were often up in the studio with the artists all night. Other than the CEO, they were the only ones who knew how to reach out to the artists directly. If I remember correctly, when I was there all the A&R reps at Motown were women. When it came to making sure things ran on time and got done at Motown, Black women were in charge and making it happen. In my experience, Motown was like *Black Panther*'s Wakanda, with strong Black female warriors. In fact, most of the people in decision-making positions were women.

After about a year at Motown, I was moved to the sales department, reporting to Oscar Fields III. Oscar was the senior vice president of sales, and he was record industry royalty. There was no one like Oscar. The best word to describe him is *impeccable*. Working for this man changed the game for me. He had a silent power about him. He commanded respect, from captains of industry as well as from the artists themselves. Oscar became my first mentor and like a surrogate father to me. He was there to teach me, and I was there to learn. He would take me to lunch, and he would explain everything to me—and I mean everything. Not only about business but life.

Oscar collected and drove only red Ferraris. His Italian suits were top of the line and the nicest suits I had ever seen. His shoes were so shiny you could see your reflection in them. At lunch, he would show me how to tip and treat the staff. We'd go to all the music industry lunch spots, like the Palm, and everyone knew

Oscar. He taught me how to read the room. When we walked in, he would make the rounds of the tables and introduce me to people. He would tell these music industry bigwigs, "Remember this guy, Stacy. He's one to watch." I felt a mixture of embarrassment and pride. At a certain point, I got the nickname Little O from people we'd meet. I wore that badge proudly.

Some of the habits I practice today, I learned from Oscar. I have always tried to pay it forward to the young people who are coming up behind me. That was Oscar's way. Oscar would get to the office very early in the morning and he would read four or five newspapers at his desk while he ate his breakfast. Once he finished reading the papers, he placed them neatly on one of the tables in his office for others to read if they were waiting for him to finish a call. He was so neat, you couldn't even tell the papers had been read. In time, Oscar started placing the papers on my desk for me to read. To this day, I read four or five papers every morning, but now I read them on my iPad.

Another thing that I learned from Oscar that I still do to this day is write personal notes to people. Oscar had personalized stationery cards, and at the end of every day he would write notes—a note thanking someone for lunch, a note along with a magazine article he thought would be of interest to someone, a note to follow up a phone call he had that day. He thought a handwritten note was more personal and would make a favorable impression. I learned to do the same. My first note cards were from the drugstore, but I remember when I felt it was time to get my own stationery. There is a famous stationery store in Manhattan called Mrs. John L. Strong. It's been around since 1929. I walked in and talked with a salesperson, working out exactly what I wanted. The cards were going to be elegant. Then I found out how much they were going to cost. I was shocked at the price, but too embarrassed to leave the shop. I asked what the minimum order was and bought what I could. Now personal stationery can be much less expensive, and I strongly encourage everyone to have some nice stationery on hand and to always write personal notes. When I have concluded a deal or if someone has had a loss or setback, I try to make sure to send them a handwritten note. Over the years, I've also developed an interest in fountain pens; I like using fountain pens because I am fond of things that are not disposable. I try to make sure things that I buy are sustainable. My two favorite workhorse fountain pens are the LAMY Safari and the Pilot Metropolitan. My favorite ink is Iroshizuku, in the color Asa-gao, a beautiful blue. Note writing is a lost art in today's digital age, but it helps maintain our humanity so much more than email or emojis.

I also learned the importance of treating everyone with respect. Oscar gave the same respect to a janitor that he gave to a multiplatinum artist. He knew the details of the lives of those who parked the cars, cleaned the floors, and answered the phones.

When we were walking out of the building, he would say to the janitor, "Hey, Frank, how's your wife doing?"

And Frank would say, "Thanks for asking, Oscar. She's doing much better. I will tell her you said hello."

Of all the things I have learned from Oscar, I feel this is the most important. Everyone you meet has value and meaning, no matter how big or small their role may seem. Treat others with the same respect you would want to be treated. Oscar had gravitas in the music industry, but he made everyone feel special. He would have a very big artist in his office and an assistant might come by to drop something off, and Oscar would stop the meeting and say to this world-famous artist, "Have you met Angela? She handles accounting and reports." And he would take the time to explain how that person's day-to-day role played a part in that artist's life.

It was an amazing gift. I have tried to emulate that trait, and I hope in some small way that I have made him proud and have done well for all the effort and time he gave to me.

In addition to those lessons, Oscar taught me the art of business travel. He would take me on trips to New York, and he knew I hadn't experienced anything like that before. But he had a way of explaining things without embarrassing me. They were little things, like how to roll-pack a suit in a suitcase or to hang my jacket in the bathroom when I took my shower in the morning so the heat and mist would press out my wrinkles. Before Oscar, I would sit in a car with my jacket on. Oscar told me that the little hook in the back seat was to hang your jacket up so it didn't get wrinkled. When we went to restaurants, Oscar showed me how to order and what the different utensils were used for. I remember we were at a lunch meeting, and we were having clams on the half shell. I was using the regular fork. From across the table, without a word and completely unnoticeable to anyone, Oscar held up this little seafood fork, and I switched right away.

These things may seem unimportant, but what he was actually trying to teach me was how to be polished, a gentleman, a good human being. He was grooming me for success. Oscar showed me that there were different worlds you had to learn to move through. He taught me that as Black men we could choose one path where we lived just in an all-Black world or one where we needed to be able to move fluidly between a Black and white world. In a Black world, you were limited. At the time, there were very few people of color who were CEOs or owned companies. It wasn't easy to find a mentor. There were limited resources and fewer opportunities. However, when you went beyond an all-Black community, the field expanded. You could get access to capital and create greater change for yourself and others. Oscar wanted to show me how to do this. He wanted to expose me to the arenas of wealth and success so that I would be comfortable and fit in any room. He wanted me to be equipped to walk shoulder to shoulder in the highest levels of the world—so that I, and others, knew that was where I belonged. This wasn't acting white or selling out. It was knowing everything about their world but never forgetting who I was. It was about gaining entry and showing people what a Black man could do.

In addition to learning so much from Oscar, there was another man who I—and so many of us—owe so much to, and that was Clarence Avant, the Black Godfather. Clarence's influence was felt beyond the music industry; it extended to Fortune 500 boardrooms and even the White House. I have always enjoyed reading biographies, and one that helped me to truly understand the type of power Clarence wielded is Dennis McDougal's *The Last Mogul: Lew Wasserman, MCA, and the Hidden History of Hollywood*. Lew and Clarence had similar trajectories. They were both kingmakers. A kingmaker is someone you may not recognize by name or face, but they run and control everything. They influence what we listen to, the images we see, and who creates those images. Even who becomes president. For Lew it was Ronald Reagan, for Clarence it was Bill Clinton and Barack Obama. There has not been a biography about Clarence published yet, but Reggie Hudlin's documentary *The Black Godfather* will give you a good idea of the man and his impact. I know in the music and film industries, almost all of us who are executives of color can trace our success and origins in one way or another back to Clarence.

Clarence epitomized the idea and the possibilities of Black ownership—ownership as in starting and running a business but also the idea of owning your career and your destiny. He believed recording artists should own their own masters (the copyright to the original sound recordings of their music) so they could reap the benefits rather than have someone else profit off their talent. In the days before Berry Gordy and Clarence Avant, Black artists often died penniless. These men helped change that.

The greatest lesson I learned from Clarence is that I had a responsibility to add to the legacy of Black success. He wanted me to always remember that if I was given the chance to play on the field as an executive or a creator, it was because I was standing on the shoulders of so many who got me there. And he instilled in me that I had a duty to give back and create space for others. I am so grateful for the gifts he imparted to me, and I will always try to live up to the ideals he embodied.

The first time I met Clarence we were working with Boyz II Men. Given Clarence's stature, you could imagine him being an intimidating figure, and if you didn't know him, you might think he was. Clarence had the demeanor of a sweet uncle, but boy did he have a foul mouth. Every third word out of Clarence's mouth was a swear word and not fit for young ears. He would absolutely curse you out, with a twinkle in his eye that said, *Don't take me too seriously, but you better do what I say.*

I always wanted to be a fly on the wall when Clarence was around. I wanted to be able to observe him and learn from him. This little tornado of a man would come walking into a room and his presence would dominate it. There was always great weight and levity in the air at the same time. It's uncommon to see this combination in powerful people. There are people you might fear or be intimidated by and some that have a fun, light spirit, but Clarence exhibited the duality. On the one hand, Clarence demanded excellence like a general at war, but on the other hand, he knew the hardships of being a Black executive and was loving and parental at the same time. He wanted you to be your best and to give your best because he wanted a good life for you and your family. He sincerely cared. And this is what made working at other jobs after my time at Motown much more difficult. All the drama wasn't necessary. It is why in future years I knew I had to be self-employed. Clarence was that influence. It was all about ownership. He pounded that into us over and over.

One of the things I admired most about Clarence was how effectively he could communicate with anyone. He could speak to and in front of white people in ways I had never seen. I'm from the South, and I was taught that you just didn't talk to white people like that and live. He spoke to a white person with the same transparency that he would with a Black person, and he would speak to a room full of Black executives and white executives without any filter. I think that was Clarence's true superpower. He was always honest. He got right down to the point and said what everyone wanted to say but they were either too politically correct or afraid to say. And he could do it in a way that no one was offended.

Years later, when I was trying to launch my own film studio, I saw Clarence at a Sony event. We caught up, and I told him I wanted to start a movie studio.

Clarence said, "Man, I have never seen one of us make it in the film game. These boys might let you act, sing, dance, and maybe direct, but owning a studio—I've never seen it. But go ahead, try!"

That response was pure Clarence. He wanted you to dream big and do big things, but he would also tell you he's never seen it and that idea you have is probably impossible. I think he knew that would just make you want to do it even more and that you were going to set your mind on accomplishing your goal. His words weren't discouraging; they were a challenge. We saw him defy the odds and make the impossible possible. He inspired us to do the same. Clarence was of the generation that was the bridge to the dreams that Martin Luther King Jr. was talking about. They were the ones creating Black wealth for the first time. They fought to get investments in the Black community. They showed the power and value of Black creativity and workmanship. Now it's my generation's time to speak that truth to today's digital power structure, who don't see the value in people of color in the C-Suite and innovation labs in this digital age. We must do our part to close the digital gap in one of the largest wealth-creation events in human history. We must have our seat at the table and be able to build tools and technology for the digital age. Right now we are small in numbers, but that is beginning to change.

CHAPTER 4

APPRENTICE RISING

WORKING WITH OSCAR allowed me to move around the company and get to know everyone. This gave me the opportunity to learn about different facets of the music industry. It also allowed me to hear when opportunities in other departments became available. Well, it just so happened that a position in the marketing department opened, and a few people suggested to me that I should apply. I went down to the office of our CEO, Jheryl Busby, and spoke to his assistant, Ruth. She was very supportive and gave me some insight on the marketing department and all the people who worked there. Ruth knew everything about everything at the company. So often people overlook the power of that position. Assistants are the gate-keepers to decision makers, and they have influence on those decision makers. Everyone you interact with should be treated with respect. That's just human decency. But you'd be wise to remember that assistants could be your greatest allies and could possibly impact your career.

Ruth let me know that she would give me a heads-up when

the time would be right for me to talk to Jheryl about the job. I made sure I was dressed up every day, waiting for my moment. Then my moment came. Ruth called me and told me to wait in the chair outside Jheryl's office while she went to speak with him. She stepped into his office and pulled the door shut behind her. I sat there, nervous, watching the lights go on and off on the big phone on her desk. A few moments later, Ruth emerged and motioned that I should go in. She smiled reassuringly and wished me luck.

Jheryl's office was much bigger than I had imagined. There were floor-to-ceiling glass windows, and the Hollywood Hills sign sat off in the distance over his right shoulder. He asked me to be seated and to give him just a moment. Jheryl had a kind, loving, fatherly disposition. He had been a very successful promotions man and had done well with New Edition while he was at MCA. Michael Bivins, one of the original members of New Edition, and later Bell Biv DeVoe, followed Jheryl over to Motown with acts like Boyz II Men, Another Bad Creation, and others. Jheryl was known for fostering young talent.

Once finished with the document in front of him, Jheryl buzzed Ruth and asked her to hold his calls, then directed his attention to me. "So, Stacy, how do you like things here at Motown?"

I gave nice answers, but he wasn't really interested in small talk. He got right to business and asked why I wanted to talk to him. I let him know that a position in the marketing department had opened up and that I would really appreciate being considered for it, and if he gave me a chance I would not let him down. He waited a beat, just looking at me, then told me that Ruth had said some good things about me and that "she tends to be a good judge of character."

He cautioned me that being a product manager was a

stressful and thankless job, with long hours and lots of hard work. A product manager managed the artists, basically the counterpart to the artists' personal managers. I never loved the phrase *product manager*. I never viewed the artist as a product. At some record labels the position was called brand manager, which was closer to what the role actually was.

I told Jheryl that I was confident that I could take on the position. He said if he gave me the job and I failed that I'd be fired, that my current job was much more secure. That made me pause for a second. I didn't want to lose my job. But I also had big dreams (fostered in part by Oscar and Clarence), and I knew if I played it safe and didn't take this chance, I would regret it. I told him I was up for the challenge and that I would not let him down. Jheryl stood up, shook my hand, and wished me luck. When I opened the door to leave, he yelled out to Ruth that he wanted Tracey Jordan on the phone. Tracey was the head of the marketing department.

"Stacy, head over to Tracey's office now," Jheryl instructed.

Now? I quickly thanked him and made my way down the hall.

As I neared Tracey's office, I could hear her on the phone telling Jheryl it was totally unfair of him to just force me on her and not give her any choice in the matter. At that moment, I almost walked away, but she looked up and saw me standing in her doorway. She slammed down the phone and muttered that she didn't like what was just done, but she didn't not like me. I'm happy to say that she eventually warmed up to me, but in the beginning, it was rocky. I was given a desk in the hall. It wasn't even a cubicle; there were no half walls, just a desk out in the open. But I didn't care; I was being given a chance.

As a new member of the department, I didn't have any artists of my own, so I was assigned the soundtracks or compilations with various artists. They were one-off projects, and I couldn't really hang my hat on them because I didn't represent the individual artists. The first project that I got was a single called "It's Wrong," which was a track about apartheid that Stevie Wonder wrote for Nelson Mandela after he got out of jail. It was going to have special packaging, and a commemorative coin would be included in a box set. I was thrilled and hoped that I could meet Mr. Wonder someday. I don't know a single Black family that didn't own Stevie's albums. *Songs in the Key of Life*, *Talking Book*, *Innervisions*—these were classics. There is just no way to explain what this man meant to the Black community and to the world. In the darkest moments of my life, all I had to do was put on *Songs in the Key of Life* and I knew everything was going to be okay. I knew I could go just one more day. It was a real privilege to work on "It's Wrong."

I was really excited about this new role, and I tried to be the first in the office and the last to leave every day. The office floor was laid out like one big doughnut. If you got lost, you'd just have to keep walking in a circle and you would find your way back again. The elevators were located right in the middle of the floor, and that's where the receptionist and the waiting area were. The artists would come in and sometimes start at Jheryl's office and then walk around to the other departments after they had said their hellos.

One particular evening, I was in the office late working on this Stevie Wonder Mandela project. I had my feet up on the desk, and I was reading a sales report. I was kind of nodding off and just needed to go home and go to bed, but I was at that point where I was almost too tired to move. The office was practically empty, so I was surprised to see two men coming around the bend. One man was leading, and the other followed behind with his hand on the first man's shoulder. The man in front gave me a 'sup nod, and then I realized the man behind him was Stevie Wonder. My head said, *Stand up, you jerk*, but when I tried to scramble to my feet, I lost my balance and fell out of the chair.

The guy in front laughed, and as they were rounding the turn up ahead, I heard Stevie say, "What was that?"

Great. I just had a chance to meet Stevie Wonder, and I fell out of my chair. It wouldn't be the last time I was starstruck, but I'm happy to say that I handled myself a bit more gracefully in the future.

I finally had an opportunity to formally meet Stevie because after the Mandela single, I was assigned to work on the soundtrack for *Jungle Fever*. This was a double honor because I was working with both Stevie Wonder and Spike Lee. It was also my first gold record. Meeting some of my idols was definitely a perk of the job.

However, sometimes it's dangerous to meet people you really admire. It's rare that they live up to your expectations. As I rose up through the ranks as a product manager, I got the chance to work on an Eddie Murphy music album called *Love's Alright*. This was Eddie's third album, following *So Happy*, which received mixed reviews and was not a commercial success. He was still one of the biggest artists in the world at the time, but his music career wasn't taking off. Many musical artists are able to make the transition to being actors, but it's much harder to go from being an actor to a musical artist. There was a lot of pressure in the company to deliver on this album, and I was in the dead center of that pressure.

Eddie had a very busy schedule, so we had to pack a lot of things into a small window of time on his calendar. Basically, we needed to get a video shot, release a single, and drop the album, all as quickly as possible. The first video from the album was going to be for a track called "Whatzupwitu," featuring Michael Jackson. Having Michael Jackson on the album was obviously a very big deal, and we hoped that this would help us get more airplay. Another plan to achieve this was to host a private album-listening party for MTV's top brass at Eddie's house. We chartered a private luxury bus to pick up Tom Freston, Judy McGrath, and others at their Times Square MTV offices and bring them to Eddie's estate, known as Bubble Hill, in Englewood, New Jersey. It was a massive home with everything from an indoor pool to a bowling alley. When we arrived, Eddie's wife, Nicole, gave us a tour and then took us to the recording studio where Eddie was waiting. After some pleasant introductions, Eddie sat down at the mixing board facing the recording booth with his back toward us. He put on a pair of dark shades and pressed play. I don't think he turned around and interacted with anyone even once during the entire playing of the album. He just jammed out, and only when it was done did he turn around and ask what we thought. Of course everyone praised it and congratulated him on the album. Then Eddie thanked them for coming, and that was it. It felt like we were dismissed. Back on the bus, everyone was quiet, but I could tell they were a bit annoyed. What was the point of the evening if Eddie wasn't even going to talk to them? Still, they did seem to appreciate the overall experience of getting to see the house.

A few weeks later, just as the first single and video were going to drop, we decided to fly all the major radio station managers and DJs to LA, since we would not be able to get Eddie to all of their markets. We set up a big meet and greet the Saturday before launch. We worked day and night coordinating travel schedules and hotel and venue arrangements.

The evening of the event, we were at the hotel and all the station managers and DJs were waiting and anticipating Eddie's arrival. We got a call that Eddie was running late but on his way. About forty minutes or so later, Eddie's long white limo arrived.

Donna Ross-Jones, his manager at the time, apologized, but we were just glad he was there. We escorted Eddie into the hotel the back way, through the kitchen, to the freight elevator. The elevator doors opened, and I walked in with Eddie, his brother Charlie, Donna, a couple of assistants, and two of the three very large bodyguards they arrived with. The elevator started to beep because we had reached weight capacity. The third bodyguard said he'd catch the next elevator, but Eddie told him to get on. Donna, who was eight or nine months pregnant, said she didn't think that would be a good idea, but Eddie insisted. The bodyguard stepped in, and the doors slowly started to close. The elevator was still beeping, as if it were crying out for help. Just when the doors were fully closed, we dropped half a floor, and the elevator alarm started ringing. Donna was not happy. A voice outside the elevator yelled down that the fire department had been called and was on its way. While we were waiting, I tried to lighten the mood by telling Eddie that MTV just agreed to put his video into heavy rotation.

Eddie looked at me and said, "Do I look like I give a fuck about that right now?"

I wanted to say, *Really? You're copping that attitude after being an hour late and then getting us stuck in this elevator because you insisted that everyone get in?* Thankfully, before I could open my mouth, Charlie Murphy started cracking jokes. Charlie was very funny and even got a laugh out of Eddie. Before long, we heard someone say they were from the LAFD and were working on things and would have us out shortly. Within minutes, we felt the elevator gently ease down to the lower floor, and the doors opened. We got off, and Eddie said he was leaving and directed everyone to go back to the limo. I begged for him to stay. I told him people flew from all over the country to meet him. Could he please stay to at least say hello? Eddie ignored me. Donna did her best to salvage the situation, but Eddie left. I had to go upstairs and let Jheryl know that Eddie was gone. He made some announcement to the room about someone being sick or something, and there was great disappointment. I don't think anyone was surprised when the album flopped.

Working on that project with Eddie gave me insight into the immense pressures that come with being a mega superstar. There's so much pressure on you and so much pressure you put on yourself to be the best and stay the best. My first thought was to be judgmental of Eddie, to think his ego was too big. But I have come to realize something different. At the time, Eddie was, by far, one of the biggest stars in the world, and he was taking a chance to try something new and different. He was following his passion for music. When you are that high up, everything you do is scrutinized. And that level of pressure has actually destroyed people. They lose the ability to innovate and take risks, suffer from anxiety and/or depression, or succumb to addiction. After working with celebrities throughout my entire career, I recognize the immense pressure that comes with living in the spotlight. Not everyone can handle it. And for those who do, it is sometimes rocky. But we should give them grace, realizing that the biggest stars are still human. All that being said, no matter how big a star you are, you should always treat everyone with respect. Others may not have had the blessings and good fortune that you've had, but they still deserve respect.

My career at Motown was taking off. By the time I was twenty-one, I was a product manager for Stevie Wonder, Spike Lee, Eddie Murphy, Boyz II Men, and Queen Latifah. If there's one artist who has had the most impact on my career, it would have to be Queen Latifah, or Dana, as she is known to her friends. She has greatly influenced where I am today.

Truthfully, it wasn't just Queen who made an impact on me

but the whole Flavor Unit family. There would be no Queen without her longtime business partner, Shakim Compere. When I started working with her, Queen had just finished recording her *Black Reign* album, and it was now moving into the marketing phase. We had to get the album and a first video done. A few years earlier, Dana's brother Lancelot was killed in a motorcycle accident. This album was dedicated to him, especially the song "Winki's Theme." Queen would go on to win a Grammy for the album. I think of all the projects I got to work on, that is the one I am most proud of.

I met Queen and Shakim for the first time at a photo shoot that we were doing in New York City. Our first location was a studio off Lafayette Street in lower Manhattan. That's where we started the day. We ended the day shooting the photo that wound up on the back of the CD box, which was taken at her brother's gravesite. This album was extra special to her.

Dana and Shakim were an amazing team. I watched how they worked together and saw that they shared a wisdom that was way beyond their years. I don't know if it was something they learned or the product of things they had been through along the way, but they knew what they were doing. I could tell she had such deep trust in Shakim, and he fiercely had her back. In business meetings, Dana could defend herself, but Shakim knew how to step in and lay ground cover for Dana in a way that didn't make her out to be the bad person. When she left the room, he had a way of having a reality check with everyone that reminded us we were all here to support Queen. I admired their bond.

Dana's mom was great too. She was Dana's rock. All the confidence you hear in songs like "U.N.I.T.Y." is from Dana being raised by a strong Black woman.

"U.N.I.T.Y." is such a great track and was groundbreaking. Queen Latifah was one of the earliest female rappers in hip-hop, and with songs like this one—which touched on top-ics of domestic violence, street harassment, and the general dis-respect of women—she was also a powerful voice for change. Dana wasn't about being a sex symbol. She demanded respect. She paved that path and made it okay for many female artists who decided they didn't want to bend to the pressure to wear less and less in music videos. She showed that a woman could keep her clothes on and still sell records and win Grammys. I was so proud to see "U.N.I.T.Y." win the 1995 Grammy for Best Rap Solo Performance and the album *Black Reign* receive such critical acclaim.

———

MY TIME AT MOTOWN had a profound effect on my life and changed my view of everything. To be immersed in a world where Black people were making decisions and running things was so inspiring. So many people believed all we could do was sing, dance, and play ball, but Motown proved to me that Black greatness went beyond that. My years at Motown were magi-cal. To get to hang out with legends like Clarence Avant, Oscar Fields, Jheryl Busby, and many more was a priceless education. And from then on, I would never believe that there was anything that we couldn't do.

While working at Motown, two ideas began to take root for me. One was that without ownership and decision-making power, Black success is limited. I worked with some phenome-nal talent at Motown, but no matter how talented, I believe that without a Black-owned company behind them, the prospects for them to grow and flourish would have been limited.

The other idea that began to take shape was the amazing things a small group of outsiders could accomplish. You didn't need an army, just a few like-minded souls set on making a difference. This was a very powerful concept to me. Up to this point, I believed the only way change could happen was to persuade the powers that be to let you in and allow you a seat at the table. But my experiences showed me that the way to really get things done was to not ask for permission or access but just do it. And that is how you can change the world.

CHAPTER 5

THE MACHINE OF MUSIC: SONY

THINGS WERE GOING really well at Motown. My office walls were filled with gold and platinum albums, and the cherry on top was the Grammy win for Latifah's *Black Reign*. What a powerful four years. And I was only twenty-five.

I guess I was making a name for myself, because I got a call from someone at Sony Music saying they were interested in my coming to work for them in their Urban division. I had a reputation for being a hard worker and now had one of the most successful product manager track records in the industry. Sony Music had always been a powerhouse. At the time, under the leadership of Don Ienner and Michele Anthony, their roster included artists like Bruce Springsteen, Nas, Cypress Hill, Pearl Jam, Alice in Chains, and more. Sony Music's main headquarters were then in New York City, and if I took the job, I would be the only Urban product manager based on the West Coast in their Santa Monica offices. But I did have to go to New York for the interview. The interview process was a series of meetings in tiny, cluttered offices that matched the personality of each person I met with. You could quickly tell the importance of each person on the team by their office: corner office, office with windows, office with no windows, assistant, no assistant. The Urban team was definitely made up of the cool kids on the block, and I felt way out of my league. One project manager in particular was so cool she intimidated me. Ashley Fox was the product manager for most of the rap artists on the label. During our meeting she was dressed in camo cargo pants, pristine Adidas, and a hoodie while I was wearing a suit, tie, and dress shoes. I felt like I looked like an insurance salesman.

One of Ashley's superpowers was evident the moment I met her: the ability to focus and drown out the outside world. Ashley's phone kept ringing the entire time I was meeting with her. Her assistant would buzz in to tell her someone important was on the line, but Ashley just told her to put the person on hold. Ashley's phone was lit up like a Christmas tree and blinking like crazy, but she paid it no mind; she just coolly sat there, taking drags from her cigarette. Finally, her assistant stuck her head in to nudge her back to the crises at hand. Ashley smiled and nodded, wished me luck, walked through the door, and returned to the world to attend to whatever fires were burning on the end of those phone lines.

You might be wondering why I even considered leaving Motown. I worked with some great acts and was surrounded by Black excellence. But I kept thinking of something Jheryl told me early on during my time at Motown. He said, "Never stay anywhere more than four years unless you have an ownership stake in the company." Those words stayed with me and drove my decision to go to Sony. I knew that I could never find another place like Motown, but I needed to continue moving forward and challenging myself to learn more about the industry. It was scary to go from being a big fish in a small pond to being a little fish in a bigger one, but I was up for the adventure.

When I accepted Sony's offer, Oscar was very upset that I didn't come to him first, but I felt if I had spoken to Oscar, he would have talked me out of going. I was truly surprised by how upset Oscar was with me for leaving. It was as if I wounded him personally with my decision. It took some time to repair that relationship. I would call and send him notes, and he didn't respond for some time. But I worked hard every day to make him proud.

Sony was very different from the world of Motown. Sony Music was broken up into different divisions. There was a division for Spanish music, classical music, album-oriented rock (soft rock), and traditional rock, for example. I was technically in what was called the Black Music division, but because of my strong background in soundtracks, I also worked across genres depending on what was required. Once a month, I had to spend a week in New York City, at the home offices at 550 Madison Avenue. When in New York, I had my own corporate apartment just two blocks from the office. At Motown, offices fit on one floor of a building. In New York, Sony had its own building with thirty-seven floors and thousands of employees. When I was there, I felt like a small gear in a giant machine.

It was infinitely easier to get things done at Motown. There, decisions were made quickly; during meetings, all the decision makers were in the same room. This was not the case at Sony. It was a very big organization, and the challenges scaled up accordingly. You had to compile updates about your artist from all the different areas of the company, write multiple reports, and wait for any decision to go up the food chain before you could get an answer. But working at Sony was a great ride.

It was the early nineties and music was changing fast. It was edgier. On the rock side, you had Nirvana, Stone Temple

Pilots, Nine Inch Nails, and Guns N' Roses. On the rap side you had Tupac, Biggie, Nas, N.W.A, and Snoop. There was also a lot of death starting to happen in music. Rappers were dying in drive-bys. Rockers were dying in crashes and by suicides and overdoses. Labels like Interscope Records, Def Jam Recordings, Geffen Records, and A&M Records were on fire. MTV was in its prime, and the industry was a wild place to be.

There was also another side of the music industry developing, an Afrocentric alternative to gangsta rap. A lot of this music was coming out of the Atlanta area. I loved the acts I got to work on while at Sony. Dionne Farris was Sony's answer to Tracy Chapman and Meshell Ndegeocello. Dionne came out of the Atlanta Arrested Development scene. This music was both old and new. It was a mix of old blues but incorporated hip-hop with a new-age R&B Afro vibe. The sound could be simple, with just guitar and vocals, or funky and complex. When you listen to tracks like "I Know" you really feel the free, folksy sound that Black artists were experimenting with at the time. I also love Dionne's rendition of "Blackbird"; it's so simple and complete. Once you heard an artist like Dionne, you loved them, but it was hard to break an artist like her into what was—and frankly still is—a very segmented market controlled by a handful of radio conglomerates. The challenge was that an artist like Dionne did not fit any specific format, and so it was harder to help her find an audience. But that was the thrill of the challenge.

MTV Unplugged was also starting to affect which artists were getting signed, what kind of sound the labels were looking for. The artist needed to be more versatile and able to do simple, intimate performance sets. On the Sony campus in Santa Monica, we would have artists do these acoustic sets to get the staff pumped up. That was something we didn't really get to do at Motown because we didn't have the space, but the Sony offices had some performance space at the offices. One of the best of these Sony acoustic sessions featured Dionne Farris and Jeff Buckley. Dionne sang "Blackbird" and Jeff Buckley performed "Hallelujah." Stop what you're doing right now pull up the acoustic version of "Hallejulah" on YouTube and tell me it's not one of the most beautiful songs you ever heard. I was standing six feet from him when he was playing, and I still hear that song in my heart. That's the power of music. I was so lucky to be a part of that.

In 1992, about a year into my time at Sony, they started a new music division called the Work Group. It was founded by former A&M and Virgin Records executive Jeff Ayeroff and Jordan Harris—I really liked those guys. I remember Jordan had one of the first electric cars—a General Motors EV1, I believe—that he kept plugged in in the garage downstairs. Jeff looked like a member of ZZ Top with a long white beard, and he was the founder of Rock the Vote. The world needs more people like those two. The Work Group, under the leadership of Jeff and Jordan, developed the careers of Jennifer Lopez, Jamiroquai, and Fiona Apple, among others.

During my time at Sony, I met some of the biggest stars and witnessed the early beginnings of others.

I remember working with an artist by the name of Trisha Covington. She had a Top 40 R&B hit in 1994 with the song "Why You Wanna Play Me Out?" and her album was produced by none other than the man who would become *American Idol* judge Randy Jackson. Randy was such a funny guy. He had a knack for delivering really bad news in such a way that you actually liked it. I've been in a room when he said to an artist, "Hey, man, you're the baddest dude in the land, but that song sucks." He was perfect for *Idol*!

Trisha had a friend who was always walking around filming her and her manager. He said he was in film school and wanted to be a filmmaker. One day, he invited me to his house. I don't think he expected me to show up, but I did. He lived in South Central at his childhood home, and I remember us sitting in his bedroom talking about his script ideas. Well, that young man was Tim Story, who directed *Barbershop*, *Fantastic Four*, and all the Kevin Hart concert films. Tim and I came up in the game together, and years later, when I started the Urbanworld Film Festival, Tim was one of the first directors to submit a film to the festival. He still likes to tease me that his first submission didn't make it in.

One day on the Sony campus, while walking to the cafeteria, I saw Michael Jackson walking in the courtyard with his A&R rep. Michael had his mask on and walked with his hands behind his back. The King of Pop was just strolling along, and as he passed, I said hello. I introduced myself and held out my hand, but instead of shaking it, he bowed down, his hands still behind him. It was such an odd moment. I told him that I came over from Motown and let him know that when I worked on the Motown twenty-fifth-anniversary *Hitsville USA* four-CD box set we had a contest, and I took winners to his childhood home in Encino, where we met with his mother.

He laughed and said, "Oh my God, did you see my bedroom?"

We spoke a bit, and I told him I appreciated his music and his contribution to the industry. What he and his family accomplished helped make it possible for me to be an executive in the music industry. He said thank you, put his white-gloved hands together as if in prayer, bowed, and walked away. Later that night I thought about the significance of meeting Michael and a thought struck me. It was about ownership again. If you have Black ownership, you can change the lives of so many people.

If Berry Gordy didn't own Motown, I probably would not have been able to have the opportunities in the industry that I was experiencing. And perhaps we would have never had a Michael Jackson or a Stevie Wonder. There had been Black recording artists long before Motown, but their ability to break out into the world and own their work was unprecedented. Yes, it was about ownership.

I think that was one of the first moments I started thinking about how I could create ownership in my life.

═══════

IN ADDITION TO WORKING with individual artists, I did the marketing for quite a few movie soundtracks. Soundtracks are different from regular albums because they're collections of artists but usually none of them are your own. Soundtracks don't tour or have screaming fans. They are compilation albums, and when they are done, your work is over. But a special one I worked on was the soundtrack for an independent film called *I Like It Like That*. The movie didn't have a big budget, but it had a Spike Lee feel to it and was a dream to work on. The movie featured the song by the same name, written by Manny Rodriguez and Tony Pabon, performed by the Blackout Allstars. If you think you don't know the song, go listen to it. I'm sure you do know it. The movie was directed by Darnell Martin and executive produced by Wendy Finerman, who won the Oscar for executive producing *Forrest Gump*. It was such an amazing experience to work alongside Wendy. She was a champion for young people in the business and fought really hard to give them a chance. She had me sit in on some very big meetings—meetings I probably didn't even belong in—where I learned a lot about negotiations and studio-level politics. The education I received on that project would serve me throughout my career.

One of the most exciting projects I worked on at Sony was the soundtrack for the first *Bad Boys* movie. I met Will Smith on the Sony lot, and Michael Bay, Don Simpson, and Jerry Bruckheimer in the studio while looking at a rough cut of the film. Everyone knew this was going to be something big and Will was going to break out with this one. I remember how we kept battling over the album cover because there was a rule that if you had guns on the cover they could not be pointed directly at the consumer; they had to be pointed off to the side or they had to be pointed down. Some retailers simply wouldn't carry an album if guns were pointing straight out. Well, the original design for the *Bad Boys* soundtrack had the guns pointing straight out. It was a cool cover, but it wasn't going to fly.

The *Bad Boys* soundtrack would become my most successful soundtrack to date. We eventually would have the number one single, the number one album, the number one video, and the number one movie all at the same time. How do you beat that?

CHAPTER 6

MIRAMAX AND THE MADMEN

BY 1995, I HAD an opportunity to move to the East Coast to work out of Sony's New York office. The industry was changing, but not in a good way. There were cutbacks at Sony Music, and a few friends—very talented people—were let go. The East Coast–West Coast hip-hop rivalry was growing. Tupac was shot (and a year later he would be killed). I remember, in one of our staff meetings, Ashley Fox strongly petitioning CEO Donnie Ienner to allow us product managers to expense Kevlar bulletproof vests and have disability insurance and hazard pay if we needed to be present at events for rappers. At the time, Ashley was representing Nas. Her concern was real. Even back when I was at Motown, two managers for Boyz II Men were shot while on tour. Khalil Rountree, the tour manager, died. But things were much worse now. Everyone was being affected by the waves of violence.

About a year earlier, Sony did some cleaning house on the movie side, and there were a series of layoffs at Columbia Pictures. Mark Gill, who was the vice president of marketing at Columbia, was phased out and went over to Miramax and became the president. I had worked with Mark when I did the marketing for a couple of soundtracks. He heard that I had moved to New York and reached out to me. He said he had an offer and wanted to know if I would consider it. I was always of the belief that it never hurt to listen to an offer, so I went to the Miramax office one night after work and met with Mark. He asked if I would be willing to come and join Miramax as the vice president of marketing.

"Of the music division?" I asked.

He said, "No, pictures." I told him I hadn't done pictures, just soundtracks, but he assured me that I could handle it, and he'd show me the ropes. He said that if I was interested, he'd want me to come back and meet with Bob and Harvey Weinstein, the two founders of the company. He told me that in addition to the big blockbuster/Oscar-contender films, Miramax wanted to go after movies that were aimed at a younger market, and these movies needed killer soundtracks. Mark knew about my success with *Bad Boys* and felt my music experience would be an asset.

I hadn't really considered leaving the music business. It's what I knew how to do. And then I thought about the meeting at Sony, where we were discussing bulletproof vests, and said sure, I would be happy to meet with the Weinsteins.

The next day I went back to the Miramax offices in the Tribeca Film Center and stood pacing in the third-floor lobby. Mark came out to get me. He smiled and said I should just relax and be myself but keep my answers brief. He led me down a short hall to Harvey's office. I was shocked at how small his office was. And the room was filled with cigarette smoke. Harvey sat behind this desk that seemed to take up at least a quarter of the space. Bob sat in one of the guest chairs in front of the desk, and there were a couple of other men in the room. Harvey wore these wide navy-blue work suspenders, and for a moment I felt like I was at a teamsters meeting.

Mark made the introductions, and I shook everyone's hand. There was no place to sit, so I just stood next to Harvey's desk. He looked me over as he took a drag from his thin Parliament cigarette, which seemed like a toothpick in his brick-like hands. I was amused when I noticed that there was an ashtray with a lit cigarette sitting on the desk next to him. Not one for small talk, Harvey jumped right to it.

"Spikes, I've heard good things about you.

"I really like Donnie Ienner at Columbia. He's a good man.

"We work hard here at Miramax. Are you interested in working hard?

"Do long hours scare you?

"We like to win. Do you like to win?"

I kept my answers short, just like Mark said: "Yes." "No." "Absolutely."

That seemed to satisfy him. He told me they had a great movie coming up and he wanted me to work on it. It was called *Scream*. He picked up a script, wiped something that looked like tomato sauce off it, and handed it to me.

"Read it and let us know by tomorrow if you want to work here."

I thanked them all for their time and made my way out of the office.

Mark walked me to the elevator, telling me he thought the meeting went great. "Call me tomorrow, and if you want it, the job is yours."

Of course I wanted the job. I knew the Weinsteins were infamous for being difficult to work for, but this seemed like a golden opportunity. At the time, Miramax was the most powerful indie studio in the world. It was founded by Bob and Harvey Weinstein and was named after their parents, Miriam and Max. Miramax had quickly risen to become a production and distribution powerhouse, and in 1993, the Walt Disney Company purchased it. The position Mark was proposing was far above anything I had imagined. Given Miramax's reputation, I knew it would be challenging, but I was ready for the challenge.

I read the script overnight and called Mark the next morning and said I'd take the job. We worked out the details, and it took about a week with lawyers to get everything hammered out. My attorney, Lisa Davis, who was also Spike Lee's attorney at the time, did a great job, and the negotiations were quick and painless. I gave my notice at Columbia. The team was happy for me. There were so few people of color behind the scenes in movie distribution that people were happy to see me getting in.

All I can say is that working at Miramax lived up to all the expectations—good and bad. Let me tell you about my first day.

The best thing that happened was in the elevator on my first day. I met the woman who would later become my wife, Marianne. I wouldn't even see her again during my time working there. It was just a brief chance encounter. That was fate.

I was shown my office by the receptionist. It was small but cozy. It was the standard setup of a desk and two chairs. It was on the third floor, and my window overlooked the Tribeca Grill restaurant on Greenwich Street. Before I even put down my bag, I got a call from Mark telling me that I was to join the rest of the marketing team in the conference room for the Monday morning staff meeting. I grabbed my notebook and pen and took off. I didn't want to be late for my first meeting.

Everyone was crowded around a long table in a small conference room. I noticed a complete AV system at one end of the room, with a large television screen, VHS, and digital tape player. As I was looking for a place to sit, I saw that there were two empty spots, one on either end of the table. Assuming these were for Bob and Harvey, I hesitated. Then I saw Mark trying to get my attention and pointing to an empty chair next to him. The entire marketing and PR teams were there. Mark pointed out a group of finance guys in the corner. Mark introduced me to everyone, and we all sat waiting for Bob and Harvey to arrive. You could hear the elevator doors open and everyone clammed up as the brothers made their way to the room. Bob looked around and noticed me.

"Eh, the new guy. Hi, new guy," he snarled. Bob sat at the farthest end of the table, where the AV equipment was, and Harvey sat at the head near the door.

Everybody else sat with their heads down; no one was making eye contact, and no one said a word. Bob was running the show. After going over the weekend grosses, he asked if some edit of a new trailer was ready. An obviously nervous person said yes and turned on the AV equipment. The trailer played, and once it was over, Bob let out a long sigh.

He said, "That's it?"

The nervous person sitting in the corner nodded.

Bob looked at me and said, "Hey, new guy, what do you think?"

I had no idea how to respond. I had a feeling of comradery with the marketing team and felt it would be best for me to be supportive of the trailer. I looked directly at Bob and confidently said, "I thought it was pretty good."

Bob slammed his fist on the table and yelled, "It sucks! It's the worst trailer I have ever seen! Are you an idiot that you would think that's a good trailer? Did we hire an idiot? Harvey, I think we hired an idiot."

Harvey, from the other end of the table with a mouth full

of bagel, said, "Spikes, did we make a mistake in hiring you? Are you an idiot?"

That was my first hour of work at Miramax.

I had seen some tough bosses, but I had come from a world where you could treat people with respect and still be successful at business. This was a management style I had never seen before; it was almost comical. However, I quickly learned to adapt to the world of Miramax. Some people at the company took Bob's and Harvey's tirades very personally and seriously, but I decided I just wasn't going to let them get to me. The only way to ever survive situations like this is to always know you can walk away and understand it won't kill you if you do. In fact, on some days when the environment was especially toxic, I would daydream about walking away.

At the time, New Line Cinema was a very big player in the urban movie space. They had box office success with *A Nightmare on Elm Street*, the *House Party* series, *Teenage Mutant Ninja Turtles*, *Menace II Society*, and *Dumb and Dumber*, and Miramax wanted a bigger piece of that market. Miramax had a division called Dimension Films that competed head-to-head with New Line Cinema. When I joined Miramax, I worked primarily on Dimension titles, given that the target demographics were young and the films often had a strong soundtrack component, which was similar to the movie soundtracks I worked on at Motown and Sony.

There was talk of Queen Latifah teaming up with Miramax to do a joint venture urban division called Miramax/Flavor. This was a hybrid unit bringing together the best of Miramax and Flavor Unit, Queen Latifah's company. We put in a lot of time trying to make this deal happen. I was on the marketing side tasked with providing backup data to support the deal. We pulled together information on the size of the urban moviegoing audience, age, spending power, frequency of attendance, types of movies, geography, storyline interests, and so much more. I was in awe of just how big this market's buying power was. The more detailed negotiations happened behind closed doors with Latifah and the Weinsteins. Given my history of working with Latifah at Motown, I naturally rooted for her success but knew there were hurdles she needed to clear. One of the dominating misconceptions in distribution circles was that Black films don't travel internationally. This meant if you had a film with a Black principal cast, it would not perform well in markets outside the United States. Now, we all knew that the three Mikes—Michael Jordan, Michael Jackson, and Mike Tyson—performed well internationally, so why wouldn't Black actors or stories travel? This unproven narrative continues to plague Black and Latino films. We have seen time and time again that good movies travel everywhere. But at the end of the day, the deal didn't happen. I was never told why, but market size and how well these films outperformed others stuck with me.

Our release slate at Miramax was insane—much larger than that of any other studio. I had more than twenty-five titles on my roster alone. It was a lot of work, but I was having some great success. That script Harvey handed to me at my interview, *Scream*, was going to be one of my first major releases. The pressure was intense. This was going to be Dimension's biggest film by far. Now that Miramax was part of the Disney family, the release was expected to have all the bells and whistles—the movie, the soundtrack, graphic novels, books, merchandise, dolls, everything. Next to *Bad Boys*, *Scream* was the most exciting project I had worked on to date. The movie was a huge success and went on to be a phenomenon, with the franchise grossing more than one billion dollars. Even more exciting than the box office receipts was seeing the Ghostface mask featured in the movie take off as a Halloween costume. It has become one of the most worn and sold costumes for Halloween in the United States since. We were able to instantly establish a new villain in the horror lexicon, and to see the movie still going strong thirty years later . . .

Miramax had a knack for using controversy to sell a movie. I remember we had a film coming out called *Priest* about a gay priest who snuck out at night and lived a double life. Miramax decided to release the film on Good Friday. Catholic groups were outraged and called for a boycott of the movie, all Miramax films, and all Disney products. They urged people to flood the Disney phone lines with angry calls if Miramax released the film. Nuns and priests joined protesters in front of our office building, picketing the movie. Walking past the angry mob on my way into the office, I wondered if they realized that all their protests were making people want to see the movie even more. They didn't understand all the free press they were giving the film.

Priest wasn't one of my films, but I did work on one that caused a lot of controversy. *Trainspotting* was a great film and an amazing project to work on. I usually didn't keep movie memorabilia from projects I worked on, but I still have my cast-autographed *Trainspotting* movie poster. The film was about a group of heroin addicts in Edinburgh, Scotland. Critics accused the movie of making heroin look sexy and fun. "Heroin chic" they called it. The craze swept music and fashion. It took the world by storm. *Trainspotting* developed a cult following. We had an entire clothing line at Urban Outfitters, with T-shirts featuring each of the characters. In record storefront windows all over the United States, we re-created the iconic bathroom scene from the movie in which Ewan McGregor's character, Renton, dives into the toilet bowl to retrieve two opium suppositories. But the best press we received wasn't of our own doing. The movie was released in August 1996, and we were in a run-up to the 1996 presidential election. Bob Dole, the Republican candidate, heard about *Trainspotting* and decided to jump on the bandwagon and vilify the movie on national television. On the campaign trail, Bob Dole held up our poster, the very one that I worked on and said that this is what's wrong with America and what's wrong with Hollywood. He railed against the movie for destroying American kids and getting them hooked on drugs, vowing that if he became president, he would clean up Hollywood. Thanks to Mr. Dole, *Trainspotting* shot up the box office charts and became a counterculture cult hit and made Ewan McGregor a star. For the record, if you watch the movie to the end, you'd see that *Trainspotting* definitely did not glorify heroin. It is one of the best cautionary films about drug use I have ever seen.

———————

I HAD A LOT of success at Miramax, but it didn't keep me out of the line of fire when it came to Bob and Harvey. I was berated, ridiculed, and insulted more times than I can count. But I wasn't being singled out. Everyone was treated the same in the pursuit of cinematic perfection. I would tell myself that we endured the behavior out of a deep love of movies and wanting to win. No one saw what we went through, but they saw our success every weekend at the box office or on Oscar night, and that high of acknowledgment and praise kept us hooked and helped us to endure the unbearable.

We used to say one year at Miramax was like seven years at any other company, and just before my one-year anniversary there, the proverbial straw was finally placed on the camel's back. As part of the *Trainspotting* campaign, I arranged for Iggy Pop— who was featured on the soundtrack and whose song "Lust for Life" was a major part of the movie—to perform on the *King*

Biscuit Flower Hour, a radio show of a live rock concert that played on Sundays and was syndicated to more than three hundred radio stations. "Lust for Life" was going to be the last song of the set and a good plug for the movie. On the day of Iggy's performance, Bob asked that I come to his office to give him an update on the *Trainspotting* project. I had just finished closing this deal, so I was feeling good walking in there. Bob was sitting at his desk, going through his briefcase. He barely looked up when I walked in.

"Sit down and tell me what's going on with the movie," he said. Bob could be cryptic and would try to throw you off by asking you to update him on a film but not be specific about which film. You had to guess which of the forty possible films he could be asking about, and if you said something other than what he was thinking, it was an excuse for him to blow up.

At least I knew what movie he was asking about that day. I confidently read through the marketing plan and finally gave him the news about the Iggy Pop show. Impressive, right? Wrong.

Bob stopped rummaging in his briefcase and looked over the top of it. "Oh yeah?" he said. "That's nice. What radio station is this *King Biscuit Flower Hour* on in the New York market?"

The Weinsteins were concert promoters in Buffalo, New York, when they first started out, and Bob had a special passion around the music side of things. For this reason, I always felt that because I came from the music industry, I had a larger-than-normal bull's-eye on my back. He would drill down on me hard when it came to anything about music. I didn't remember the station off the top of my head and definitely didn't want to get it wrong, so I told him I had the spreadsheet with the listing of the radio stations, which was sitting on my desk. I got up to go get it when he let loose.

"YOU DON'T KNOW?" Bob yelled. "How can you not know what station it's on in New York? Are you kidding me?

Get out of my office." He screamed for his assistant to have me removed and that I should never be allowed back in his office because I was a waste of space.

Bob's assistant gave me that smile and shoulder shrug combo he gave a hundred times a day. I walked back to my office and made a decision. That was it. I was done. I just couldn't take it anymore. But I had the wherewithal to call one of my buddies to let one person know that I was of sound mind and body for what I was about to do. I got Ed on the phone. He always loved my insane Miramax stories.

"How's hell today?" Ed asked.

"Well, Ed, I've had enough."

Ed chuckled and asked if I was finally going to quit.

"No. I've decided I am going to kill Bob Weinstein," I admitted.

Now Ed laughed heartily and then waited for me to laugh back. I didn't laugh back. I told him I just wanted to call someone and let them know what I was going to do and that I would gladly spend my life behind bars for the pleasure of killing Bob Weinstein.

"Oh, I see," Ed said, "and how do you plan to do it?"

"I am going to kill him with my BIC pen."

"I see," Ed said again. "And when are you planning on committing this crime?"

"In a few minutes. As soon as we hang up."

"Stacy, have you eaten today?" Ed asked.

What the hell does that have to do with the fact that I am about to kill Bob Weinstein?

"Stacy, will you do me one favor before you kill Bob? Please go eat a sandwich."

"What are you talking about, Ed? Eat a sandwich?"

"Stacy, just go eat a sandwich and call me back before you kill Bob. Okay?"

I went to the deli across the street and sat down at one of the little black two-top tables and ate a sandwich with chips and an orange juice. After the sandwich, I felt less homicidal, and needless to say, I didn't kill Bob Weinstein. But I did decide I had to leave Miramax.

I believed that I would probably just go back to the music industry, but before I had the chance to put out some feelers, I got a call from John Schmidt, the former CFO of Miramax who was now at October Films. An independent film production company founded by Bingham Ray and Jeff Lipsky in 1991, it was then being run by Ray, Schmidt, and Amir Malin. October billed itself in the independent world as the more filmmaker-friendly distribution company as compared to Miramax. Bingham would often tell filmmakers that at October Films they'd have final cut of their film, but at Miramax, Harvey Scissorhands would. John asked me if I would be willing to meet with them about heading up their marketing division. Bingham wanted me to come to a screening of a Lars von Trier film they were planning to release called *Breaking the Waves*. We met at a screening room in Midtown. Bingham had a very straightforward way of operating that I would come to see him employ many times. He would just put all his cards on the table. And he had this way of speaking to someone; he would lean in very close to your face and put a hand on your shoulder and look you right in the eyes. At the screening he told me that he wanted me to watch this film that he thought could win the Oscar for Best Actress and he wanted me to help them achieve that.

If you haven't had a chance to see *Breaking the Waves*, you really should make a plan to see it. There are times when you watch a movie and when it ends your world will never be the same—your view of life is permanently altered. *Breaking the Waves* did this to me. Emily Watson portrays a young woman who falls in love and marries an oil rigger who, just a week after their wedding, gets injured and is paralyzed from the neck down. Emily's character hears God's voice, and you don't know if she is crazy or gifted. By the end you know. Emily's performance is just brilliant.

After the movie ended, I just sat there for a moment. Then Bingham turned to me, and right there on the spot I said, "I'll do it." I told him I would leave Miramax and come to October Films to help release this film because I thought it was so amazing and I believed Watson could win the Oscar.

There was one small problem. Harvey was notoriously competitive when it came to staff leaving. Regardless of how he treated us, he viewed us as his team, and you didn't leave to join the competition—especially not October Films. I approached Mark Gill, who was my direct supervisor, and was straight with him. I told him I was going to October Films to be the head of their marketing department. Notice I didn't say I had gotten an offer; I presented it as a done deal. I didn't want Miramax to counter; I don't know if they even would have. But I had already decided I wanted out.

Mark was sincerely happy for me but acknowledged that we'd have to figure out what to tell Harvey. He knew he'd flip out. After thinking for about a minute or two, Mark decided he'd just say I was going back to the music industry. I told Mark I trusted him to do whatever he thought was best. A couple of days later, Mark called me into his office and said I was good to go. I thanked him profusely. He was truly a great boss, and I would never forget his graciousness and generosity. I knew that eventually he was going to take a lot of heat for that lie. Mark Gill was a rare breed of man. He never lost his cool or displayed any of the trickle-down behavior that you can often find in toxic work environments. Mark would take bullets for his team. He was always the last to leave the office, and he looked out for us. I will never forget how Mark handled situations under pressure. Back then I swore that if I was ever a leader, I would try to protect my team the way Mark did. I hope I have lived up to that promise.

A few weeks later, I started at October Films. Their offices were located on the second floor of a building just off Bleecker Street near Lafayette Street in the NoHo area of Manhattan. On my first day, all the major trade publications announced my arrival at October Films. That's when all hell broke loose. About midday, there was suddenly a loud commotion down the hall. I could hear Bingham and John yelling. At first, I thought the two of them were fighting, until I realized they were arguing with someone else. It was Harvey. Bingham put Harvey on speakerphone and turned the volume up so the entire office could hear.

Harvey raged, "You stole one of my best people, Bingham! I'm gonna make you pay. You open one movie, I'm gonna open four the same day. You shouldn't have crossed me. He was one of our best."

I was sitting in my office listening and just shaking my head.

While Harvey was in the middle of his tirade, Bingham appeared in my office doorway and leaned in on the frame. "Are you hearing this?" he asked. "He must have really liked you."

I laughed and told him that a week before I left, he told me I should get the word *idiot* tattooed on my forehead so that in the morning when I looked in the mirror, I would remember what I was. Bingham guffawed and went back to his office. Harvey was still going.

"Bingham, I was letting you exist before this, but now I am going to buy all the movies and I'll leave you nothing."

Bingham picked up the receiver and said, "Oh, Harvey, shut

up," and slammed down the phone. The whole office applauded. That was my first day at October Films.

THE AWARD SEASON was fast approaching, and we were hitting the ground running with *Breaking the Waves*. We had the two main members of the cast, Emily Watson and Stellan Skarsgård, to book for interviews and PR.

The way the award process works is you must have your film play in at least Los Angeles and New York City for one week in order to be qualified to compete in the Oscars held at the beginning of the following year. Then you had to make the academy aware of the film with ads in magazines and on billboards, as well as sending videotapes of the movie to the voting members of the academy branches that you wish to influence. You would also design beautiful booklets about your film and send those to the members as well.

We fought hard and were able to get a Best Actress nomination for Emily. We were very proud. But the Oscar wound up going to Frances McDormand for *Fargo*. We couldn't be mad at that. She was great in that role.

AROUND THIS TIME, Sundance was the most important film festival around, and films showcased there were hot commodities for all the movie companies. The battles between Harvey and Bingham started to become legendary. Usually after a screening of a film, Harvey would hold court in one Park City restaurant, and Bingham was in another across the street. Filmmakers would ping-pong back and forth, listening to the pitches for what would happen with their film if they signed with each company. Harvey would promise that he would make you into the biggest director there was; he would say that he hoped you liked winning Oscars because you were going to bring home at least two or three. Then the filmmaker would make their way over to Bingham. He didn't make big promises, and he had only one arrow in his quiver. He actually played Harvey against himself. Against his reputation for being difficult.

Sometimes it worked, and sometimes it didn't.

There's an old saying that goes, "If the movie is successful, congratulate the director. If the movie isn't successful, blame the marketing." Now that I was the head of marketing, the responsibility rested on my shoulders. For the most part, it can be a thankless job. The Academy of Motion Picture Arts and Sciences grants awards for the best director, actor, actress, producer, writer, special effects, makeup, but nothing for the marketing or the publicity of a film. We are invisible. In my opinion, if the artwork, trailer, marketing, and publicity aren't done right, you can have a great film and it will never get seen. This is a shout-out to all my fellow marketers. I see you, and if no one has told you today, I think you're important and doing an awesome job.

In my role, I was on the front lines of the fights with the producers and directors of the films. In their minds, they have made the greatest film of all time and the world needs to know about it. Ads here, billboards there—anything to get their "baby" the attention it deserves. But we had budgets we had to stick to. And at October, we prided ourselves on being frugal. At Miramax, we spared no expense when it came to marketing, but now I needed to be mindful of the bottom line.

I got into one particularly heated exchange with Bill Paxton while working on *Traveller*, a film he produced and starred in alongside Mark Wahlberg and Julianna Margulies. We had taken the film down to South by Southwest (SXSW) and were getting good traction as we neared launch. Bill called me and wanted to discuss the marketing campaign. He was being very complimentary and sharing some great stories about the production of the film. I got out the financial report because I knew he was going to ask me for something, I just didn't know what it was yet. I politely listened, and then he lowered the boom.

In his southern drawl Bill said, "Stacy, we need a billboard on Sunset Boulevard."

A billboard on Sunset? Did he have any idea how much that would cost? That's one of the hottest pieces of advertising real estate. He told me all the ways this billboard was going to be great for the film, but looking at my budget, I knew there was no way it could happen. It's not uncommon in Hollywood to place billboard ads. We have even gone so far as to make sure to have those billboards located near the home or office of the director or star. It's an ego thing. This was and still is a common practice. But this film just didn't have the budget for it.

Bill and I went around and around, and I finally said that if Bingham or John or Amir wanted to give him a billboard on Sunset it's fine by me, but he'd have to take it up with them. Then he started to get mean. He was yelling, calling me names, and getting himself more and more worked up.

I really didn't care for his tone and some of the things he was saying, so I calmly and kindly said, "Hey, Bill, why don't you call me back after you've calmed down?" and hung up the phone.

Well, I guess Bill didn't hear my final words and thought I just hung up on him, so he proceeded to flip over his desk and destroy his office. I don't remember if he got his billboard or not, but if he did, it didn't come from my budget. We kissed and made up at the movie premiere; he apologized for getting all worked up, and I said it was all good. He wasn't the first filmmaker to yell at me, and he wouldn't be the last. The higher up you climb in the social hierarchy, the more you will deal with the hard decisions that have to get made and the unhappy people on the other side of those decisions. You are usually telling someone who has worked on a project for years they are not going to get something that they have always envisioned or thought they deserved. This is hard, but I have found it's best just to deliver the information straight and make room for their reaction. I also try to propose they come back with any alternative ideas they might have. This usually allows the person to go off and calm down and speak to others on their team, which helps them get some perspective.

I *was* asked to rent a billboard for David Lynch's *Lost Highway*. October Films was growing, and this was our biggest release to date. David lived up in the Hollywood Hills, and the billboard sat just off La Cienega in a prime location. Working with David was great. The thing about genius is that they see something and are willing to go to any lengths to get the rest of the world to see that vision too.

I remember sitting in David's house and we spent a couple of hours talking about what shade of yellow the highway line on the movie key art needed to be. The tiniest detail received his full attention, and he wouldn't settle for anything less than perfect. He wasn't a demanding prima donna; in fact, David was extremely laid-back, always meditating, just very chill. But he had an artistic vision, and everybody respected that. Working with him was one of the highlights of my time at October Films.

CHAPTER 7

BAPTISM BY FIRE: URBANWORLD

W HILE I WAS still at Miramax, I started to realize how large but underserved the Black movie market was. When we were trying to get Miramax/Flavor off the ground, we had the numbers in black and white. For example, in the year 2000, Spike Lee's film *The Original Kings of Comedy* had a production budget of $3 million and grossed $38 million, which was a twelvefold profit. *Castaway*, a Tom Hanks film released the same year, had a production budget of $90 million and grossed $429 million, which was just a 4.7-fold profit. In addition, urban films tended to have higher per-screen profit averages. *The Original Kings of Comedy* was released on 847 screens, with a per-screen average of $13,051, and *Castaway* was released on 2,700 screens, with a per-screen average of $10,412.

There were a handful of Black actors who were box office draws: Denzel Washington, Wesley Snipes, Eddie Murphy, Angela Bassett. And a small stable of directors.

Being one of the few people of color in movie distribution, I was featured in a few Black magazines—*Ebony*, *Jet*, *Vibe*,

Black Enterprise. And this exposure inspired quite a few let-
ters from people asking if I could help them with a project. It
would either be an idea for a film, a script, or an actual finished
film. I'd regularly get VHS tapes in the mail, along with a note
asking me to help them with their film or if I could give them
some advice. I tried to answer all the mail, but it almost became
another full-time job. However, it made me realize that I had a
responsibility to help. I needed to do something. At Sundance
and other film festivals, I noticed there just weren't any Black
people and there were hardly any Black films.

It was an ambitious undertaking, but driven by passion and

I met with the director of Sundance at the time, Geoff Gil-
more, in his Santa Monica offices on one of my trips to LA. We
chatted for a bit, and I actually asked him why there weren't more
Black movies at Sundance. Geoff gave me a speech about the
thousands of submissions they get every year and if there were
more good films they would show them. *Good according to who?*
I wondered. *There's a lot of good work out there.* I left that meeting
so angry, and I really have to thank Geoff because it was that
conversation that pushed me to create a festival for us and by us.
I didn't think it was fair, and I couldn't just sit at my desk in the
hottest studio on the planet at the time and do nothing. God
didn't bring me that far to not try to help others. It was my duty.
And standing outside the Sundance offices I determined I was
going to make a Black Sundance Film Festival.

It was an ambitious undertaking, but driven by passion and
indignation, I was unstoppable. I reached out to some like-
minded people who I thought could help me. Producer Helena
Echegoyen, Miles Ferguson, and Ariel Peretz joined me in starting a planning team. I went to my friends Keith Clinkscales and
Len Burnett at *Vibe* and had a chat with them. The working title
I had for the project was the Black Market Film Festival. Keith,
who was the *Vibe* CEO, didn't think that worked.

"Hey, brother, I really love where you're going, but it's not about Black or white. It's about *urban*. It's about a state of mind," Keith said in the jazzy smooth way he talks.

"Urban?" I asked.

He went on to explain how it was not about race but mindset and culture and where those things meet. He said it's about the urban world, those melting pots where cultures collide. And it should be for all those who don't have the same access as the elite, who have to make their own way by any means necessary. A place where people from different backgrounds can come to know one another and share their different cultures. He said it was like when you mix hip-hop and karate movies and get Wu-Tang.

I got it. Keith knew what he was talking about. And I trusted him. Under his leadership, *Vibe* magazine had surpassed *Rolling Stone* in sales. He was the king of the music magazine universe. Every *Vibe* magazine cover was a work of art, as good as *Vogue* or *Vanity Fair*.

Keith said, "The right name will come to you." Well, it already had. He had already said it. It was the *urban world*. And that's what we went with. The reason we combined the words *urban* and *world* was because we could not trademark the words separately, but when we combined the words and made them one we were able to trademark it. Urbanworld was born.

Keith and Len agreed to beta test the concept of an urban film festival, but at that time the Black music conferences were the big thing. There was Jack the Rapper, C. M. J., How Can I Be Down, the Vibe Music Seminar, and a few others. These were massive conferences. *Vibe* held its conference at the Waldorf Astoria in New York.

So, we made a deal that we would have a music panel on soundtracks and show one movie during the Vibe Music

Seminar that year, and if the response was good, *Vibe* would come on as partners to do Urbanworld the following year.

I worked hard trying to put everything together at night after I came home from work and on the weekends. During this time, I transitioned from Miramax to October Films, but Urbanworld was my baby, and I kept at it.

The film we picked to screen was *Set It Off*, starring Queen Latifah, Jada Pinkett, Vivica A. Fox, and Kimberly Elise, and directed by F. Gary Gray. *Set It Off* is still one of my favorite movies, with what I think is one of the best death scenes in cinema. When Cleo (Latifah) dies in the scene with her '62 Impala Lowrider Sports Coupe, the crowd lost their minds. You have never seen a film until you've seen a movie like *Set It Off* with an all-Black audience. The screening was so over capacity, people were seated in the aisles and standing along the walls. If it was a fire hazard, the managers were very cool about it because they wanted to see the film do well.

Everyone was so proud of the movie, and it was an instant masterpiece. It accurately depicted the times and where society was and what we had all experienced with the deaths of Tupac and Biggie. It was both a commentary and release valve on the whole subject matter.

Following the success of the screening, Keith and Len agreed to sponsor and support the first Urbanworld Film Festival, which would be held in conjunction with the 1997 Vibe Music Seminar. We had a simple deal. They would help with sponsorship and promote the festival as part of their conference, but we would operate as a stand-alone conference that people could register for and attend separately from the music conference. However, there would be a special deal if you signed up with the *Vibe* all-access pass; then you were able to attend both conferences.

Once we had the backing of *Vibe*, I started running around

town making calls for possible sponsors, and we caught a lucky break in the form of a woman who would be our hero for many years to come. Olivia Smashum was a soft-spoken but powerful woman who was head of affiliate marketing and business development at HBO. We had a nickname on the street for HBO: Home of Black Opportunity. HBO and the Warner Brothers systems lived up to that nickname with not only the content that WB, New Line, and HBO made but also the executives they hired and promoted. HBO and the Warner family put their money where their mouth was more than any other studio in the industry. When you walked into an HBO meeting, you saw Black and brown faces, and they weren't only assistants; they were the decision makers.

Olivia agreed to meet with us, and I have to be honest, I was very nervous. Olivia was the type of person you just couldn't read in a meeting. She had a solid poker face. Olivia didn't smile or anything. She just wanted the facts and for you to get to the point. I pitched the idea of the Urbanworld Film Festival to Olivia and her team and then held my breath. She said nothing for a full minute, and I thought for sure it was a no-go.

But then Olivia said, "HBO is committed to helping Black and brown stories to be seen and heard. I think you have a good idea, and we are willing to support you. I will look at my budgets and see what we will be able to do."

True to her word, Olivia called the following week and said they would be sponsors of the first Urbanworld Film Festival. I believe the first check was for about $5,000. We had our first sponsor. As I write this, I have to say that HBO has been a sponsor of Urbanworld for twenty-five years straight, and their role and commitment to Black and brown voices in front of or behind the camera cannot be overstated. They have made an astounding difference in the lives of so many and were mavericks in creating a safe space for those new voices. I am deeply grateful for all HBO has done over the years and thank all the individuals who played a part.

There was a lot to be done to pull everything together, and it seemed like that year passed by quickly. We were able to find a single-screen theater to host the event. It was right next door to Radio City Music Hall on Fiftieth Street in midtown Manhattan. This was prime real estate and a great find. We had one small problem: the manager seemed like such a sweet guy, but let's just say that he would become a different person after he had his liquid lunch. And this "different person" wasn't fond of people of color. Dealing with racist people wasn't new, but this man was the epitome of Jekyll and Hyde. He seemed perfectly normal before he started drinking, but if you spoke to him in the afternoon, he became a blatantly racist person. Our team had many conversations about just walking away from this theater and refusing to work with this man, but it wasn't quite that simple. We couldn't just find another space because there were so few single-screen options in the city. Plus, we needed to be within walking distance of the Waldorf Astoria so that we could benefit from the Vibe Music Conference foot traffic. Refusing to work with this racist would hurt us more than it would hurt him. So we figured a way to just work around him. We would do our calls with him before noon, and if he tried to call us later in the day we would wait until the next morning to call him back. Let me give you an example. I happened to be on the phone with this gentleman to discuss the contract one afternoon. It was obvious from his slurring that he had a few drinks in him, and he started asking some rather offensive questions. We had not met in person, so I suspect he didn't realize I was Black.

He asked me in a sharp tone, "What kind of people are you

inviting to this festival? What do you mean by *urban*? Does that mean colored people? Is this a festival for Negros?"

I kept my cool and said that the festival would be open to the public and anyone could attend.

He said, "Oh, okay, well, that's okay, then."

Growing up in the South, I knew people just like this man. That's why he didn't rattle me, and I knew how to deal with him. In the future, we let Joy Wong, the film festival's executive producer, deal with him. She was a powerhouse who whipped everyone into shape. There was no way that festival could have happened without Joy. She was superhuman in so many ways. I don't know how she did it. She organized the teams, did the program book, the film schedule, everything. Because of Joy I was able to sleep at night.

We wanted Urbanworld to be different from other film festivals. Being in New York City, we wanted to capture the energy and diversity that you find in major cities. We wanted a melting pot of topics and conversations among all people. There were a handful of us executives of color who would attend the other major festivals. We referred to ourselves as the raisins in the milk. Back then, diversity wasn't as mainstream as it is now, and these festivals had just sprinklings of diversity around the edges. They were able to check the box and show that they had representation, but the festivals were not designed to deeply include filmmakers or audiences of color. We dreamed that one day Urbanworld could be a festival that looked more like the actual moviegoing audience, which included all colors and backgrounds. And we could allow all creative voices to be able to express themselves and see their communities and stories on the big screen. In 2010, the *Daily News* called Urbanworld "The People's Festival" because of the inclusive and community nature of our festival.

Our submission guidelines said if you consider yourself a

filmmaker of color, you could submit any work. If you were not a filmmaker of color, your film's principal cast would need to include people of color. Films that did not have studio distribution could participate in competition. A film was not eligible to compete if it had already aired on television or had a theatrical run. We wanted the festival to be international and showcase films from all over the world. Africa, India, Japan, Sweden, and more could be represented. Calls for submissions ran in *Vibe* magazine and the *Hollywood Reporter*. We had no idea how many submissions we were going to get that first year, but the response was amazing. The second bedroom in my apartment had hundreds of VHS tapes piled up in it. Against one wall I stacked movies that had not yet been seen. The wall across from that had three piles: yeses, noes, and maybes. Every night after work and on the weekends, all I did was watch movies. I was amazed at the content I was seeing, the worlds I was able to visit. Even the movies in the no pile were remarkable. The effort I saw from these filmmakers was so incredible. One of the films, which came to us from Africa, took the filmmaker ten years to complete. I remember there was a scene that had no building in the background and then suddenly there was a building there. I came to find out that it took the filmmaker two years to save up more money to complete the film, and in that time a building was constructed on the location where he filmed. Regardless of the inconsistency, the filmmaker's drive to tell his story was inspiring. I knew we were creating something special with this festival; we were amplifying voices by giving these films a home.

The dates and the film slate for the festival were finally locked. The opening night film was going to be *Hoodlum*, starring Laurence Fishburne and Andy Garcia. Closing night was going to feature *Soul Food*, starring another all-star cast that included Vivica A. Fox and Vanessa Williams, and executive produced by Babyface and Tracey Edmonds.

—————

THE THING ABOUT FESTIVALS—and I guess you could say life itself—is that things always go wrong. Our first festival was no exception.

Back then, websites were not as prevalent, so you still sent out mailers to potential attendees. The mailer would give highlights of the festival and entice someone to attend. Our first mailer was a forty thousand–piece run. I went to our printers, XL Graphics, to inspect the run. Ever since my days at American Video, I loved being on press during a run, watching a job come to life. So the run was almost done, and given the humidity they were going to let it dry over the weekend. Then on Monday they would send it to the sorting company downstairs, who would address the mailers, add postage, and take them to the post office.

While we were standing there admiring the work, one of the staff members came up and said, "Doesn't Laurence Fishburne have an *e* on the end of his name?"

I felt my stomach drop. *Oh God, please tell me we did not misspell Laurence Fishburne's name.* Michelle, who worked in the office, went over to the computer, looked it up, and yes, we forgot to put an *e* at the end of Mr. Fishburne's name. By this time, all forty thousand mailers had been run. Naturally, when something like this happens, all sorts of absurd apocalyptic ideas begin running around your head. *I'm ruined. I'll be sued. I will go bankrupt. The studio will pull the film.*

Jeff, the owner, saw my despair, laughed, slapped me on the back, and said, "Don't worry about it. We'll figure something out." They reran the job for me at a huge discount. That would not be the last time my friends at XL saved me. The one thing I've learned over the years is no matter how careful you are, mistakes will happen, and it is very important to be kind to your vendors because there will come a time that you will need their support. I've seen far too many colleagues who were disrespectful to vendors, and when they needed help there was none to be found. Always treat your vendors with respect.

We jumped that hurdle, and things seemed to get back on track. We had the films we would screen locked in. We had gotten the program book done. We had posters and badges and all the things you need to make a festival happen. Now it was showtime. The opening-night screening of *Hoodlum* was taking place at a theater on the east side of Manhattan. The theater was arranged by the studio United Artists. Rain was predicted, and as I started getting dressed to make my way there, the rain started coming down in sheets. I knew we were doomed. Who was going to show up on a night like this? I sadly got into a taxi and made my way to the theater. I knew I had to rally and put on an upbeat front for the staff and the studio, but to be honest, I was just gutted that our festival was going to be a disaster.

As the taxi pulled up to the theater, I could see a few people standing in the rain waiting to get in. I asked the driver to go around the block. I wanted to see how long the line was. I was astounded when I saw the crowd. There had to be three hundred or four hundred people standing in the rain. We were sold out! I jumped out of the taxi near the back of the line and started walking along, thanking everyone for coming. I assured them that we would let them into the theater momentarily, and everyone was patient and kind.

When I got into the theater, I could feel that the atmosphere was electric. I saw Joy and we both smiled. We were actually going to pull this thing off! We let the guests in and had an amazing opening-night premiere. It was all a blur, but I never forgot how I felt seeing everyone standing in the rain to attend something we created. For the first time in my life, I was no longer an outsider, a guest in someone else's world. There is an immense gratification that comes from seeing a hard-fought dream realized.

As was the plan, our festival was integrated with the Vibe Music Seminar, whose panels were taking place at the Waldorf Astoria. So, the next night, we headed over there for our panels. As we—the Urbanworld staff, filmmakers, and actors of color—stepped from town cars and taxis toward the Waldorf's golden doors, we were met with beaming smiles of our brothers who were doormen welcoming us with pride and honor. We were the embodiment of a dream that so many had, that so many worked hard to fulfill. We were creating a place for ourselves, a place at a table that had traditionally been closed off to people of color. We were breaking barriers, and our voices were being heard. We still had a long way to go, but you could see our accomplishment in their eyes.

I had come specifically for the panel on soundtracks. If my memory serves me correctly, brother Bill Stephney, who was the president of Def Jam Records and had signed Public Enemy, was moderating the panel. I walked into the ballroom and saw five hundred seats filled with Black and brown faces. The room was filled with Black hip-hop power. I don't know if the Waldorf had ever seen that many Black people who were not there to carry bags or serve food.

Once the panel was done, I had to get back to the single-screen theater and make sure everything was going okay. The next few days were long, but all went smoothly. Attendance was great, and there was electricity in the air. The Guild 50th Street Theater lobby was filled with filmmakers, actors, and producers in deep conversations sharing their odyssey in filmmaking.

Filmmaking is an endurance sport. Like life, it's so important to show up, try, and just not give up. I want to tell you a story about something I saw at our first festival that has always stayed with me as a lesson of the importance of never giving up.

One of the films that was in competition for Best Picture that year was called *A Woman Like That*, directed by David E. Talbert. Dave was a gospel play stage director from Las Vegas. Gospel plays are like Broadway for the Black community, and if you have the opportunity, seeing one of these traveling plays is an event that you do not want to miss. The Black gospel plays include the best of church, drama, comedy, and suspense all in one. Dave was an up-and-coming star in this arena and decided to spread his wings and make one of his plays into a movie.

A Woman Like That had one of the evening showcase slots, and we would have tech run-throughs for the films before their screening time. Dave and the producers arrived at the theater, and we realized we had a big problem. The film was what was known as an unmarried print. This means there are two separate prints—one with the picture and the other with the sound. The projector we had could only run a print with the picture and sound married to a single piece of film. Our projectionist tried to solve the problem. Projectionists are such a special breed, and there are not many around today. To get a sense of what a projectionist does, check out the film *Cinema Paradiso*. A good projectionist has an unyielding sense of perfection, striving to make sure that the audience experiences the film exactly how the director intended it to be seen. They are responsible for the brightness of the light bulb. The sound levels. The transitions from the previews to the feature. Making sure the film starts on time. Today all of this is done with digital files that run on digital projectors, but during our first film festival, technology was not there to save Dave or his film.

Our projectionist made a few calls and let us know that he

had found a sound-only projector, but there would be a risk that the picture and sound would be out of sync. He told us how much it would cost to rent the projector and asked if we wanted to give it a try or cancel the screening. I agreed to cover the cost of the projector if Dave wanted to take the risk. He enthusiastically said let's go for it.

We got the projector delivered, and we were testing while the audience was lined up outside.

I could see the projectionist's discomfort, and he just kept saying, "I don't know, I don't know."

Dave was a champ and said we should just let the people in and give it a try.

We got the audience in and seated. You could tell they were excited. It's fun to see how different films attract different audiences, and this was a beautiful crowd. It was a mixture of church-going people and regular folks, but everyone was very appreciative and knew this was a special event. Not only were films like this rarely made but they also didn't usually have premieres at a film festival either. The cast was all in attendance. I introduced Dave to the stage, and I could tell he was a little nervous. This was the first time his first film was going to screen. He introduced the cast and let everyone know that this was a working print and asked them to please forgive any technical difficulties.

The crowd gave Dave an amazing round of applause as the lights went down and the curtains opened. Some of us ran up to the booth while others stayed in the back, holding our breath. We got through the first few minutes of the film with no problem, but then you could see the sound starting to slip. The characters' lips were moving, but the sound was delayed. The projectionist tried to tweak it by hand, but then the words were heard ahead of the image. I was in the booth watching the projectionist wrestle with the film with one hand on the knob that controlled the speed while he looked out the view window to the screen. The crowd began to laugh, some tried to shush them, but they laughed anyway. Some began to boo. I don't know who that hurt more, Dave or the projectionist. Neither wanted to let the crowd down.

We stopped and restarted the film two times. It kept getting worse. Dave decided to stop the film. He bravely stood in front of the crowd and apologized. The audience applauded him, and the spirit leaving the theater was upbeat, but I could see the pain in Dave's face as he stood in the lobby thanking people for coming.

The following day I saw Dave and his team in front of the theater. They let me know that they decided that they were going to go back to Las Vegas early. The award ceremony was on Sunday, but given the disaster of a night they just had, they figured they would save on the hotel cost and just head home. I said I understood but reminded them that the film jury sees the films on video, not at the screening, so they were not aware of what happened at the theater; they would base their decision on what they saw on tape. Dave considered this and decided to stay and see what happened.

On Sunday morning, everyone gathered for the award ceremony. The mood was festive but tense. As we made our way through the awards, I could see Dave check his watch frequently. He seemed detached from the proceedings, like he was just waiting for it to be over so he could leave. After what I am sure seemed like forever, we had finally arrived at the award for Best Picture. The presenter stood at the podium and said it was a very difficult choice for the jury. The competition was tough, and it was hard for them to pick one winner. The presenter commended all the filmmakers, saying they were all winners simply because they completed something many will dream of but very few will ever do. Then the winner for Best Picture was announced: *A Woman Like That*, directed by Dave E. Talbert.

Dave and his team leaped up in shock. Dave made his way to the podium and rehashed the horror, disappointment, and pain he felt over the failed screening. He could not believe they had won. He thanked God and his family as he raised his award to the sky.

I share that story because no matter how bad you feel, it's important to show up anyway. There's a saying I love: "Don't quit before the miracle." So many times, we give up at the very moment things are about to change and we never see the promise of possibilities because we gave up and went home. Don't quit. Being an outsider, if you are going to win, you have to have staying power well above those who don't have to work as hard or as long as you will need to. So stay the course and eventually you will hit land. Dave continues to make movies to this day. He has been back to the festival several times to premiere his other films and loves telling this story to the crowd before the lights go down.

CHAPTER 8

OWNERSHIP MATTERS

I SLEPT LIKE A STONE that Sunday night following the festival. I was back at my desk at October Films Monday morning. At a little after 10:00 a.m., Bingham showed up in my doorway with a newspaper in his hand. He asked how my weekend was. I said good, tiring but good, and asked about his.

He said his was fine, and then he held up the paper and said, "Looks like you had a busy weekend." He turned the paper around to show me a big article on Urbanworld.

"Yeah, the festival went well," I said.

I noticed Bingham couldn't look me in the eye. He folded the paper and, staring at the floor, asked, "Do you think you can do this and your job at the same time?"

I said, "Of course, why not?"

He just stood there, leaning on the doorjamb, looking down at the floor with his arms folded across his chest. The silence was loud.

I said, "Bingham, you sit on several boards and give your time to film-related charities. How is this different? If I don't start a festival to help filmmakers of color, who will?"

He straightened up, unfolded his arms, and said, "Well, now I know why that last movie failed. You're distracted." With that, he walked away.

At that moment, I knew they were not going to renew my contract and I was going to be out of a job. And a month later I was out. Not having a contract renewed is an interesting thing. You're not fired, but you don't have a job. Well, if I am honest with myself, I *was* fired. I sat at home sulking for a few days, but then I got a call from Trina Wyatt, who was the CFO of the Tribeca Film Center. She asked me to meet her for lunch. We met at the Tribeca Grill, which was right downstairs from her office. Trina asked all about the festival and was very complimentary about what we had achieved in such a short amount of time. She asked how things were at October Films, and I said I had left and was taking some time off. That's the slick way of saying I was unemployed.

Trina had this bouncy personality, and no matter what you said, she would respond, "Oh WOW! That's great." After some small talk, she said that the reason she asked me to lunch was to know if I was interested in the Tribeca Film Center becoming a sponsor of Urbanworld. She said they were really impressed with what we were doing and wanted to be supportive. Her offer was cash sponsorship and the use of half an office rent-free for three months. I sat there stunned.

She said, "Well, what do you think?"

Of course, I said yes.

It was a great opportunity for Urbanworld, but what was I going to do? I thought about this on the subway ride back to my apartment. Do I look for another marketing job at a movie studio? Do I go back to the music industry? I had little motivation to do either. What really excited me, what really made me feel like I had purpose, was the work I was doing with Urbanworld. As I told Bingham, I had to help filmmakers of color. I felt like it was my calling. I created it out of nothing, and at that moment, I truly felt like it was the most important thing I had ever done in my life. I thought about the fact that most founders are created after they get fired or when there is a downturn in the economy, and though I had founded Urbanworld while I had a job, maybe this was the time to devote myself to it fully. At that moment, I decided I never wanted another person to have control over my destiny. If I was going to fail, I wanted to fail trying to do what *I* wanted to do. Life is hard enough, so I may as well live my days following my dreams and trying to make a difference in the world in the way I believed I could best serve it.

I showed up at the Tribeca Film Center the following week and was shown to my new office. It was the perfect room for new beginnings. I now spent all my time working on the festival—getting set up as a nonprofit, chasing sponsorship dollars, and putting in long hours. As we got closer to our second festival, I had to bring on some help. I asked Trina if they could provide a bigger office, and they were able to give me one that would accommodate three people. We crammed five people in there. I was finally able to draw a salary, and we had four other part- and full-time employees. We couldn't pay much, but everyone was committed to our mission to make a difference.

We took everything we learned from the last festival and were determined to make this one even better. But not everything was smooth sailing. When we printed a mailer to get people to register, I checked everything carefully before it went out. I double-checked the spelling of everyone's names. No more misspellings. Everything looked perfect. The mailers went out on a Thursday, and I expected we would start getting calls for registration in two or three days. Well, early the next Monday morning, I was sitting in the office alone when the phone rang.

I answered, "Hello, Urbanworld. Can I help you?"

A very distraught woman's voice on the other end of the line said, "Is this Urbanworld? I insist on speaking to someone in charge immediately."

I told her I was the founder of the festival and asked what I could do to help her.

"I am completely and utterly disgusted that your 1-800 number is a live phone-sex line. Is this some joke? Because if it is, it is in very poor taste."

I apologized, but she had to be mistaken. We'd had the same phone line for two years now.

I asked if I could put her on hold, but she simply said, "Sir, you have filth on your phone line!" and hung up.

She had to have dialed wrong. I grabbed one of the mailers from the stack on my desk. I dialed the number very slowly, saying the numbers out loud as I dialed. The line rang, and then I heard it: a breathy voice said, "If you want it bad, come and get it good. You've reached 1-800 Love. . . ." I quickly hung up and dialed the number again. The same breathy voice. *No, no, no, God, no.* I put the phone down slowly and screamed. Sixty-five thousand of those mailers went out, and radio stations and news outlets would be posting that 1-800 number on their websites. We were so screwed. I broke out into a sweat and called Susan Jacobs, our publicist. I told her about this disaster, and to my utter dismay, she burst out laughing.

"Susan, this is not funny!" I yelled.

She tried to compose herself and told me not to worry. She said she would call me back in a few minutes.

Thirty minutes later—the longest thirty minutes of my

life—Susan called back and said she'd taken care of it. Took care of it? I asked her what she did.

"I have a piece that's going to run on Page Six in the *Daily News* tomorrow."

What? Susan assured me that it was good PR, but I was a wreck. The next morning, I grabbed the *Daily News* from the newsstand in front of my apartment and turned to Page Six. There it was, a juicy gossip piece about our 1-800 number being switched with a phone sex line. I wasn't sure how this was going to help us, and we still had sixty-five thousand mailers that directed people to call a sex line out there. I got on a call with Susan, and she said I should just call the company that owned the phone number and have them forward the line to our correct number. After some wrangling, the company agreed, and we worked it out. It took about a week to get fixed, and enough people called the line and heard the message that it became a bit of a joke. When I walked the red carpet for the opening night, every interviewer wanted to talk about that phone line. Even the filmmakers told the story of what they heard when they called the Urbanworld 1-800 number. It's now part of Urbanworld folklore. Where were you when you heard the Urbanworld sexy phone line?

That experience taught me the importance of not taking myself too seriously. Mistakes are going to happen; things are not always going to go as planned. So many things are out of your control—even when you're a founder. The best advice I can give you is: try your best, and when the inevitable bump in the road happens, keep your sense of humor about it.

———

NOW THAT URBANWORLD was my full-time job, my number one priority was bringing in sponsorship dollars. I needed money to be able to pay my bills, and I needed to pay our employees. But there were other things to be done.

We were no longer running the festival in conjunction with the Vibe Music Seminar. *Vibe* continued to be a sponsor, but we went independent because we had outgrown being a part of the music seminar. And that meant we had to figure out our place in the festival calendar. Sundance ran from January to February. Cannes was in May. The Venice Film Festival was in August. The Toronto Film Festival was in early September, and the New York Film Festival was in late September. We could have gone with sometime in spring, but after much discussion with the team, we agreed that late August/early September was the best time for us. Why? Well, historically, Black and Latino movies had the strongest presence in September and October. Yes, there were some Black and Latino movies in the Thanksgiving season and again in February for Black History Month, but early fall had the strongest showing. The August/September window helped us to be competitive with some of the major festivals and would also make the festival serve as a launching pad for urban titles releasing in the fall. We needed to premiere films two to six weeks prior to their theatrical release in order for the festival to be considered a source of critical exposure by the studios. If the Urbanworld Film Festival was going to be the biggest home for Black and Latino titles, we needed to fight for our position.

Being in New York City was also key. New York was an easy destination for filmmakers and media. Some larger media outlets might send talent to Sundance, but a lot of them were based in or around the New York market, so our location gave the films a much better chance at PR exposure.

We also needed to secure a theater space. We couldn't go back to the theater by Radio City Musical Hall. We needed more screens, and there was no way we were going back to deal with that guy. Manhattan is one of the most expensive theater markets in the world, and it is hard to find space. But I immediately thought of someone who could help. My former colleague Jack Foley was head of distribution at both Miramax and October Films. If anyone could find us a space, it was him. Jack knew everyone in the industry. But what I admired most about him was his cool and calm demeanor. He was like Teflon; no matter what craziness was going on around him, it would just slide right off him. I remember one time I was sitting in his office at Miramax when his phone rang. He answered and put it on speaker.

A female voice said, "Jack, I have Harvey for you."

The call was patched through, and we could hear a deep drag on a cigarette followed by a long exhale. This is the conversation that ensued:

> HARVEY: Jack, why do we only have fifteen hundred screens booked for this release?
>
> JACK: Because that's what we can get right now. That film is not going to play higher.
>
> HARVEY: Are you a fucking idiot? This film should be on at least three thousand screens.
>
> JACK: Harvey, it's not going to happen.
>
> HARVEY: Jack, are you that incapable of doing your job? Are you so stupid that you can't book one of the best films ever created, Jack? Does the chairman of the company have to do your job for you?

Jack looked up at me, grinning.

> JACK: Harvey, you're dreaming; it's never going to happen. Now, I'm in a meeting. I'll have to call you back.

Jack hung up just as Harvey was starting to lose it.

Jack leaned back in his chair, locking his fingers behind his head, and said, "What a blowhard," then with a big smile on his face resumed talking to me like nothing had happened, as if he had just gotten off the phone with Mary Poppins or Mother Teresa, not Attila the Hun. I couldn't believe how he could just shake Harvey off like that. This is why I loved Jack. He has one of the coolest, most positive attitudes of anyone I have ever worked with in the industry.

So, when we needed to find a theater for Urbanworld, I called Jack. Jack said to give him a few days and he'd call me back with a couple of options, and true to his word he called me in two days. He said I should go see Travis Reid, the CEO of Loews Cineplex. Loews was one of the large theater chains that later merged with AMC to become the largest theater circuit in the world.

A meeting was arranged with Travis's office. When I arrived for the meeting, I was shown into a large conference room. Eventually, three executives entered, introduced themselves, and sat at the large mahogany table that dominated the room. The chair at the head of the table nearest the conference room doors sat empty, presumably for Travis. The group was not very chatty, and seemed to have no idea what we were all doing there. Travis walked in, apologized for being late, and greeted me with a firm, hearty handshake. He was tall, with the type of frame that a well-made business suit dreams to hang from. He had salt-and-pepper hair, wire-framed glasses, and a boxed goatee. He had a commanding presence.

Instead of taking a seat, Travis said, "I have to return to a meeting. Stacy is a friend and colleague of Jack Foley, so he is a friend of ours. He's launched a film festival that needs a new home. Please take care of him and give him what he needs, okay?"

Then he looked at each of the three executives, waiting for their nods of understanding.

After they each confirmed they had heard his orders, he said thank you and walked out.

The woman across the table sat up tall and said, "Well, I have never seen Travis do that before, so you must be very special. How can we help?"

Travis has been one of my biggest mentors and supporters of my career ever since. There is no way I would be where I am today without the key actions that he took. If you ask anyone about Travis, you will hear people say he is one of the good guys, and I wholeheartedly agree.

On your journey, be on the lookout for those special angels who seem to be put in your path to assist you. They can be anywhere. Nothing happens without mentors or helpers. And always let them know how much you appreciate them. If you have an event, invite them. If you make a product, share it with them. Make sure to let them see what they played a part in creating. My twist on John F. Kennedy's quote is: failure is an orphan, but success has a thousand parents.

After that initial meeting, we made a deal that the festival would take place at the Loews at the Worldwide Plaza, which was located on Fiftieth Street between Eighth and Ninth Avenues. What was so unique about this theater is that it was completely subterranean. You would have to take these escalators down underground to get to the theater. At the time, it was a six-screen dollar-house theater showing second-run movies, and it was perfect for us. We took over the whole theater. Second-run films were movies that were months into their run and played at a much cheaper price compared to opening weekend. There are very few of these theaters left. The industry shifted away from this model.

At that second festival we had a stellar lineup. On opening night, we had *Why Do Fools Fall in Love*—the Frankie Lymon story starring Larenz Tate and Halle Berry. The spotlight film was *How Stella Got Her Groove Back*, starring Angela Bassett and Taye Diggs, and on closing night we were showing *Down in the Delta*, Maya Angelou's directorial debut starring Alfre Woodard. This festival also brought two people into my orbit who reaffirmed my calling to commit myself to Urbanworld and its mission.

We had a film in the festival called *Classified X*, which is a French-US documentary about the history of Black cinema narrated by Melvin Van Peebles. It is very well done and comprehensive, and I encourage you to check it out. You can watch it on YouTube for free. We had decided we wanted to give Melvin a lifetime achievement award.

Because we were only in our second year, he didn't know about us and what we stood for. He asked to meet with me to learn about Urbanworld and to discuss this award. Melvin lived just two blocks from the theater, so I graciously accepted the invitation to go to his home. When I arrived, Melvin answered the door wearing trousers, no shirt, and suspenders. He had on these psychedelic purple specs and held an unlit cigar in his mouth.

He said, "Come on in, youngblood, and close the door behind you."

His apartment had a bohemian vibe, with walls of deep purple and blue. Soft jazz was playing in the background. He motioned for me to take a seat and then just started grilling me, firing questions one after the other, trying to determine what I knew and didn't know about the history of Black cinema. Luckily, I had seen his movie and could hold my own, but at a certain point, I surrendered. There was a lot more I didn't know.

I realized he wanted to teach and for me to learn.

He said, "You see, youngblood, the mission we are on is

important. We are trying to educate people and change the world." He talked about his appreciation for the French, and Europeans in general, and how they had more respect and appreciation for Black artists. He dropped knowledge about what he and other Black rebel filmmakers had to do to make movies. How they didn't have distribution. The pages of our cinematic history were coming to life with his words. Melvin kept rolling along, jumping from topic to topic, film to film, trying to pass on all he knew. He spoke quickly and with passion, as if he had to impart all of this wisdom before the stroke of some hour when he would disappear and all he knew would vanish with him.

How fortunate I was to sit at the knee of this legend and learn all that came before us to forge the path forward. We sat together talking for more than five hours. We didn't eat. We didn't drink. He just talked, and I sat and listened. And then it was over.

He stood up and said, "All right, I'll accept your award. Now get outta here, youngblood."

I left that apartment floating on air, with a new appreciation of the filmmakers I had the honor of working with. Receiving the oral history of a struggle is so important, and to be able to spend time talking to the ones who were there is invaluable.

Melvin came to the award ceremony, and I think it made him very proud to see this busy hive of Black and brown faces working so hard to carry on what he and so many others had fought for. We were the manifestation of their labor and sacrifice. It was our way to say *Thank you, we are grateful for what you did for us, and your legacy is strong in us.* Every time I am faced with a challenge and am attempting to make it to higher ground, I always imagine those who came before me watching and rooting me on, and I don't ever want to let them down.

I HAVE MET A LOT of famous people in my life, but one of
my biggest thrills was meeting Maya Angelou. We were so lucky
to host the world premiere of her film *Down in the Delta*, and
even luckier to have her and the cast attend. I was thrilled. I had
seen Dr. Angelou on television and video but had never met her
in person. Her words—poems like "Caged Bird" and my favorite,
"Still I Rise"—have had a significant impact on me. The latter is
the ultimate tale of perseverance in the face of the deepest adver-
sity. That poem has buoyed me up through dark times and given
me strength when I couldn't find any of my own.

I don't know about the rest of the team, but I was very nervous about meeting Dr. Angelou. I had the kind of fear you have
when you genuinely want to make a good impression and you
know you have only one shot. To me, Dr. Angelou was Black
royalty. She was a bridge spanning the river between those who
fought for civil rights and us, their beneficiaries. Getting to meet
her would truly be an honor; I felt as if she was coming to see
how we were handling our inheritance.

When Dr. Angelou arrived, I greeted her at the rear of the
theater as the excited crowd waited inside. She was so warm and
genuine, and she had a presence about her that demanded respect.
Being around her made me want to stand tall and straight; I
wanted to make her proud.

I gave Dr. Angelou a rundown of how the evening would go:
I would introduce her. She would then introduce the cast and say
a few words. Then we would begin the film.

She said, "That's fine, baby, that's fine," and I suddenly felt
completely at ease.

I gave the staff a heads-up that we were ready to roll and
made my way down to the front of the theater. I was greeted with
applause.

I introduced Dr. Angelou, and the crowd went wild. They

leaped to their feet and gave her a thunderous round of applause. Dr. Angelou made her way down the middle aisle of the theater as eager fans reached out to her. We had Sym, our head of security, accompanying her, but she graciously shook hands and smiled as she walked to the front of the theater.

When she reached the stage, I handed her the mic and stepped aside so I could be a part of the audience and delight in her presentation. The applause continued, and no one sat down. She looked out over the sea of faces and began to speak as only she can.

"Look at you, and all of your beautiful faces. I am so honored to be with you tonight. Thank you for having me and my cast. This is my first film, and I hope there will be many more. This festival you all have created is so important. What you are doing here is needed. The world is hungry for this. We need to see ourselves on that screen. We need to tell our own stories. Do you hear me? We must do it. 'Cause if we don't, who will? There is nothing like an idea whose time has come, and Urbanworld's time has come."

The crowd roared. To have Dr. Angelou declare the importance of what we were doing with Urbanworld was a life-changing moment. If I'd had any doubts about the importance of this mission, they evaporated completely. I was doing exactly what I needed to do. It brought to mind the final lines of her poem "Still I Rise." I was using the gifts my ancestors gave me and living out their hopes and dreams. I was giving voice to people of color, past and present, and paving the way for the future.

CHAPTER 9

URBANWORLD TO THE WORLD

OVER THE YEARS the festival grew, and we were looking at ways to do more. We wanted to find ways to expand the brand and do more year-round activities. This would allow us to grow and generate more revenue. In one of our staff meetings, we discussed taking the best of the festival on the road. A traveling version of the festival. We eventually settled on the idea of visiting historically Black colleges and universities, and other universities that had film schools.

We were really into the idea of reaching a younger demographic, but would there be any interest from the schools, and would we be able to find someone to sponsor the tour? We reached out to some of the HBCUs to see if there would be interest in such a tour, and the response was very strong. Several of the schools had films screened on their campuses to promote a studio film release, but none of the schools had ever hosted a traveling film festival. At the time, universities were a strong area of focus for brands and media companies. MTV had MTVU, which was a version of the station that was focused on the college market. We looked at MTVU's activations on campuses and figured we could have similar activations using film rather than music.

After we had finished another successful annual festival and the dust had cleared, we formed a general idea of how the tour would work and what the format would be. We put a budget together and decided we needed to test it out on a potential anchor sponsor. I took the idea to Olivia Smashum, who was our main contact at HBO. Since HBO was the presenting sponsor of the festival, we figured it was the best place to start, and the team at HBO always supported new and bold ideas. Olivia liked the idea but said she needed to get back to me. During our next visit, she came back with some disappointing news: the price tag was too high, and she did not have it in her budget. I think she was as disappointed as I was.

But I wasn't ready to give up yet. Bill Jancosko, one of my mentors, whom I had met at a private equity firm in Colorado while raising capital, taught me that when raising money or sponsorship dollars, you need to do all your homework before you walk in the door. One tip he shared was to read the annual and quarterly filings of the company if it was publicly traded, to see if you were headed in the right direction. If you're in the apple business and the company is getting into the orange business, you might be wasting your time. So, following Bill's advice, prior to visiting Olivia I had read all the quarterly and annual filings for AOL Time Warner (HBO's parent company) over the last couple of years. One of the things constantly mentioned in all the filings was that most new subscribers to HBO were young people just out of college who had gotten their first apartments. I mentioned this to Olivia in our meeting. She tilted her head and asked how I knew this. I told her about what I read in the public filings from the last couple of years.

She smiled slyly and said she had an idea and would get back to me as soon as she could.

A few weeks later, Olivia called and said our budget for the tour had been approved and AOL Time Warner and its brands wanted to be the exclusive sponsors. Bill was right: always read the filing documents. I've made sure to do that in all my business dealings.

Olivia's news was amazing, but I also panicked a bit. I was grateful we had funding for the tour, but now we had to make it happen. Our goal was to kick off our tour just after Martin Luther King Jr. weekend. To make our target date, we had to book and be on the tour in less than sixty days. An added wrinkle was that all the schools were doing finals and would adjourn for the season in two weeks. There was a lot to do, but we had a great team, and I knew we'd figure it out. We had to build out the website with tour dates and activities on each campus. We had a program booklet that we had to produce. Of course, we had to book the specific venue on each campus and do a tech rider, which details the equipment needed at each venue to ensure we had the right setup. We had to drop-ship gift bags to each of the locations. Book all the hotel dates. We were going to take an RV rather than fly, so we had to get the RV graphically wrapped. We had to set up press interviews in each market and determine if the surrounding community could attend or if the dates would be open to students only. These were just some of the details.

––––––––

IT WAS THE LAST week of January, and we were in an RV with the Urbanworld and HBO logos on the side, making our way to our first college of the tour. The little secret that I couldn't tell any of the sponsors was that we had less than half of the tour fully booked at this point. I was on the phone in the back of the

RV booking dates as we made our way down the highway. Sometimes you have to forge ahead to make things happen. Rarely is everything laid out perfectly in advance. You have to trust that you will be able to figure things out as you go along.

My parents both graduated from an HBCU, so it was really exciting to be able to do this tour and visit these institutions that have served great Black minds. However, I had no idea what a profound education I would receive by doing this. We wound up doing two separate tours, about a year apart. On the first tour Tony Murphy and Van Groove traveled with me, and on the second, Tony Murphy and Andre Lee accompanied me. Tony had been our festival programmer from the very beginning and has worked on the festival consistently more than any other person in the organization. Van Groove was a friend of the festival and a DJ. Andre worked on the festival and at one point was my assistant.

The format of the program was that I would address an assembly of students early in the day, and while I was speaking, Tony would go to the venue and get the tech check for the film we would show in the evening. Van Groove would go to the campus station to promote our upcoming event. I would usually give a lecture about the movie industry, followed by a Q&A. These were a lot of fun.

I did my best not to make the movie industry sound too glamorous. I apologize now to any parents whose children switched from a more respectable major to chase dreams of show business.

Each campus was very special in its own way. No two were the same. Sometimes we had discussions after the screenings late into the night, standing in front of the venue long after it was locked and most had gone home. In Atlanta, we had one major event hosted by Clark, Morehouse, and Spelman. They launched the evening with a step show that you would not believe. Stepping was developed in the mid-twentieth century by African American fraternities as a display of pride, strength, and unity. Blending African folk tradition with popular culture, these synchronized dances involve stomping, clapping, and body slapping, resulting in a drumlike syncopated rhythm. Such dancing can actually be found throughout history in different cultures all around the world. You can even find similar tribal war dances like the haka, which originated in the nineteenth century in New Zealand with the Maori tribe, being done today before rugby matches. The Atlanta show was perfect, done with military precision, and was met with roaring standing ovations from the crowd. You owe it to yourself to experience a step show at an HBCU. It's both moving and powerful and transcends words.

Doing the college tour had meaning that I was not able to understand at that time. I thought we were trying to expand the Urbanworld brand and look for additional ways of driving revenue for the company. This was true, but in hindsight I realize we were arming the next generation with the knowledge that film could be a form of civil and social activism. We were teaching them that there was power in their stories being told using this visual medium. Our parents and grandparents fought using song and marching. Now we live in a world where visual storytelling is king, and it is important that they know that power. If not, they will be left without a voice. We were helping to lay the groundwork for the storytellers of the future. We gave them the tools and encouraged them, affirming that the stories they wanted to tell were important and they needed to tell them with brave and committed hearts. Because if they didn't, who would?

On our second tour we screened an HBO documentary called *Murder on a Sunday Morning*. It's about Brenton Butler, a fifteen-year-old kid who was walking to the store in Jacksonville, Florida, to fill out a job application. A police car stops him and asks him if he can come to a crime scene. Once there, a distraught man whose wife had been shot claims that Brenton was the shooter. The boy was not allowed an attorney, was beaten, tried as an adult, and found guilty, even though he was innocent. It was a powerful film and sparked many impassioned conversations. We all know this story far too well. Many of the students could see themselves in Brenton. Many had their own stories to tell.

After each screening, we would have town hall–style meetings where we would have judges, police officers, and academics available to answer questions. These were tough but important conversations, and everyone appreciated the movie and the fact that we were bringing such an important topic to the surface for dialogue. These conversations were healing, and it wasn't uncommon to see students and police officers weeping and hugging each other after the event. These programs changed perceptions and changed lives, and I was very proud that we could help make that happen.

HBO was hoping to get an Oscar nomination for the movie, and we were part of their ground campaign. The day after our program at Xavier University in New Orleans, I received an early-morning call informing me that the Oscar nominations were just announced and *Murder* was nominated. The tour suddenly took on a totally different meaning. We wanted to do what we could to bring awareness to the film and its impact to drive thought, conversations, and change. The attendance at the events was already great, but now we were being moved to much bigger venues on campus, and the events were completely sold out. Now every city we went to had local news crews waiting to interview us about the film. The HBO PR machine had kicked into high gear. It was very exciting.

A few months later, I was at home watching the Oscars on

television along with the rest of the nation. When the envelope was opened and they said the winner for Best Documentary was *Murder on a Sunday Morning*, all I could do was weep. I felt so honored and blessed that we got to take that special film to those colleges and have all those town hall meetings, and I was grateful that the academy and the world outside of Black communities recognized the importance of it as well. I wish I could say that the subject matter is no longer relevant, that it is merely a sad part of history, but as we know, we continue to see this type of injustice. The Urbanworld Film Festival continues to be a launching pad for works that shine a light on racism, persecution, and social and environmental inequality. We are very proud of our history of supporting documentary filmmaking in this area and its impact. These are the best films in the world about hard-hitting subjects and are often being made by filmmakers who come from the areas that are most affected.

═══════

OUR FIRST URBANWORLD tours were a success, and it was so gratifying to be able to bring these diverse films to a wider audience. It made us want to do more, to reach more people, to give these amazing creators an even larger platform, and there were still a lot of independent films that were not making it to the market. The internet was a new frontier, and we saw that a lot of the hip-hop nation was rushing to make a land grab. Given that we had some excellent traction with audiences around the country thanks to the tours, we decided to launch a distribution company that would release urban films to the market and make them available online. There was a push for online streaming services at this time, but none were able to gain traction because the user experience was still too poor given the low bandwidth. It could take twenty minutes to download a digital video file of a movie that was the size of a Post-it and very grainy. But everyone could see the future was coming, and we were all rushing to be first. One of the leading players in the space was a company called Atom Films. They focused on Oscar-winning short films. They were purely online movies. Our business model was unique for the time. Our plan was to release a movie a month theatrically, and if a person went to see the film in the theater, they would also have access to see the movie online for free. If they did not see the film in theaters, they would be able to rent it online once it was made available.

Looking back, we were a little too early with this concept given that internet speeds were still very slow and watching a movie wasn't a smooth experience. But the promise of high-speed streaming capabilities was just around the corner.

Still, the rush to stake a claim in the digital world was on. We had amazing content to share, but we needed a pipeline, a platform for people to watch it on. At the time, there was a Black and Latino sector of the internet bubble, and there were several companies jockeying for consumer attention: Hookt, Volume .com, 360HipHop, BET.com, IndiePlanet, Black Planet, and so many more. There was also a company called Urban Box Office—UBO—founded by George Jackson, Frank Cooper, and Adam Kidron. I knew George and Frank, who were alums of Motown.

UBO had deals with everyone. One of the deals they touted at the time was with Venus and Serena Williams. Flush with cash, UBO was on a rapid buying spree. Given that Urbanworld had a decent profile, I shouldn't have been surprised when I was contacted by George Jackson to meet to discuss the possibility of UBO buying Urbanworld. I went over to their impressive offices. They probably had about two hundred employees at the time. George walked me around, introducing me to all these Black and

If there is one lesson I've learned, it's this: It really doesn't matter whether you succeed or fail, as long as you are willing to try. In trying, you just might make it.
Courtesy of Urbanworld Foundation Inc.

My mother, Rose, with me (*right*) and my brother, Marcus.
Courtesy of the author

Me with my father and brother when the family came to visit me in LA.
Courtesy of the author

We weren't sure how many people would show up for the first Urbanworld Film Festival,
but we had a great crowd.
Courtesy of Urbanworld Foundation Inc.

Our first Urbanworld award ceremony was held at the Waldorf Astoria.
Courtesy of Urbanworld Foundation Inc.

Me and Melvin Van Peebles after we gave him a lifetime achievement award.
Getting to learn about our collective history from him was a profound experience. We owe him a lot.
Courtesy of Urbanworld Foundation Inc.

Maya Angelou at the Urbanworld Film Festival premiering her directorial debut, *Down in the Delta*.
Courtesy of Urbanworld Foundation Inc.

The tour bus we used to do our first Urbanworld HBCU tour in 1999.
Courtesy of Urbanworld Foundation Inc.

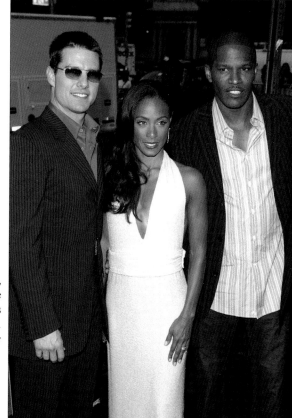

Tom Cruise, Jada Pinkett Smith, and Jamie Foxx at the premiere of *Collateral*, one of Urbanworld's biggest premieres.
Peter Kramer—Getty Images

When Hamet Watt and I launched MoviePass.
Liz Hafalia—Getty Images

The very first active MoviePass card.
Courtesy of the author

A MoviePass billboard in Times Square, 2018.
Courtesy of the author

Announcing the launch of MoviePass 2.0, February 2022.
Lawrence Miner Jr.—Courtesy of MoviOne Inc.

brown kids doing their thing. The offices had all the swag you would expect. Finally, George cut to the chase: "So how much would you *sell* Urbanworld for? You should come and join us. We are it and the place to be."

George was very well-known in our circles. He was a heavy hitter, the producer of films such as *Krush Groove, Jason's Lyric*, and *New Jack City*. The fact that he wanted Urbanworld was huge. I heard George out.

His pitch was simple: "We have money, we are going to be big, and you should join us now before it's too late."

We never discussed hard numbers, but he said I should think about it and get back to him quickly if I was interested.

It was a lot to think about. Being part of UBO had its upside. I liked the idea of not needing to raise capital, and Urbanworld Films would have an amazing platform. It would be a featured UBO.net brand, and I would still be able to run it, but UBO would have complete control of the brand. Something just didn't feel right to me. It felt risky. And there was something impersonal about George's offer. It was not that he wasn't sincere, but it felt like it was just business to him. I could tell he saw Urbanworld as a good investment, but if the deal didn't work out, he would just move on to the next opportunity. It felt like it really didn't matter to him if he bought us or not. But for me, Urbanworld was everything. I wasn't interested in signing it all away. I decided to wait a week or so to see if George would reach out. I wanted to see if he was hungry for us. But I didn't hear from him. I often look back at that moment and wonder if I should have sold Urbanworld. Should I have taken the money and run? Perhaps, but something told me to hold on to what we had and keep growing it. Urbanworld had a strong brand. There's no science to this, and sometimes if you have shareholders, your hand can be forced to sell. Urbanworld had no investors, so we could decide to wait until the right fit came along.

A few weeks later, George had a stroke and died suddenly. He and his wife, Yuko, had a daughter, Kuna, who couldn't have been more than one or two at the time. It was so sad. Everyone from hip-hop and the urban tech scene was at the funeral. His death changed the urban tech scene instantly. When George died, it was as if the heart and soul of UBO stopped. UBO would collapse in two years.

Around this time, Sony restructured its music division and spun off Sony Digital and named Fred Ehrlich its president and CEO. Fred was GM of Columbia Records when I was there. The entire music industry was being shaken up by Napster, a peer-to-peer internet music-file-sharing program that allowed consumers to download music for free. To accelerate Sony's race to grab its part of the internet, they created an incubator called 550 Digital Media Ventures, an investment arm focusing on digital technology.

I got an audience with Fred and his team to pitch them. The first meeting went well, but things were going slow. Fred was constantly flying off to Japan, and there could be weeks between meetings. However, it seemed like we were getting close to an investment.

I was in constant contact with Fred's office to stay on his calendar and try to close. One afternoon around five, I got a call from Gerri in Fred's office. She asked if I was available to meet with Fred that night at seven o'clock because he was leaving for Japan the next day. I told her I had an appointment that evening but would try to move it. She asked that I get back to her quickly because there were others who were trying to meet with Fred. I actually had a commitment at a church event that night, and it was something I felt I could easily blow off, but something held me back from just canceling. I decided to check in with my spiritual mentor, a man by the name of Van. I called Van and explained the situation, figuring he would tell me to go chase the money because that was most important, but that is not what he said. What he did say was life-altering.

He said, "If you want to achieve great things in life, you must always remember to honor your first commitment, no matter how big or how small."

He then said, "I am sure you will make the right decision," and hung up.

His words echoed in my head. *Always honor your first commitment, no matter how big or how small.*

Arrgggg! My heart raced. What was I going to do? The clock was ticking, and I knew I didn't have that much time to contemplate my decision. I wanted to follow Van's suggestion, but I thought it was completely foolish. I tried to find a loophole in what he was saying. Honor your first commitment except when it comes to money? No, that didn't sound right, but it didn't make sense to pass up this chance to have dinner with Fred. I knew I could close the deal at this meeting. As Van's words echoed in my brain, another piece of wisdom entered my head. General Norman Schwarzkopf famously said, "The truth of the matter is, you always know the right thing to do. The hard part is doing it."

I dialed Gerri back. As soon as I said hello she started rattling off where I should meet Fred. I stopped her mid-sentence by saying, "Gerri, I won't be able to break my commitment this evening. Please tell Fred I'm sorry and I look forward to being able to meet with him upon his return."

We had become friendly over these months of my meeting with Fred, and I knew she had my best interests at heart when she said, "Stacy, do you know what you are doing? I have no idea when I am going to be able to get you in again. If you want to meet with Fred, you really should do it tonight."

I thanked her for her concern and asked her to let me know his next availability upon his return. Gerri sighed deeply and said she would do her best, but he had a very heavy travel calendar for some time into the future.

After I hung up, I sighed deeply too. What did I just do? I saw Van a couple of hours later at church, and he patted me on the back, telling me, "When you do the right thing, things work out right."

I was not reassured.

A couple of weeks later, Gerri rang me and put me on Fred's calendar. We were to have an eight o'clock breakfast on the top floor of the Sony building. I had worked in that building for years and had never been to the top floor. When I got off the elevator on the thirty-seventh floor, I was met by a security guard who bowed and showed me to the room where we would be dining. It was as if I had entered another world. I was instructed to take off my shoes and leave them on the mat outside the door. Inside, the room was very simple in the classic Japanese style. I was directed to sit at the horigotatsu-style table in the middle of the room. The table was set low to the ground, and there was a recess under-neath it for your legs, so basically you are sitting on the floor. I had just gotten myself situated when the door opened and in came Fred. He quickly slid himself into place and motioned for an attendant to bring us some tea.

Fred was always a direct person, and the first words out of his mouth were, "So, what was so important that you stood me up last month?"

I nearly choked on my tea, but quickly composed myself. I sat up tall and simply said, "I made a commitment that I needed to honor." Then I braced for impact.

Fred said, "Well, that's why I invited you to breakfast. I want to let you know that we have made the decision to invest in your company. We want to be involved with founders who stand by their word and honor their commitments. Integrity is very important to us."

Van had a very good laugh when I told him what happened.

———

WE WERE ABLE to get Urbanworld Films off and running. We staffed up and started acquiring movie rights. We also received an investment from *Black Enterprise* magazine, and they did a photo shoot and featured me on the cover. That was a big honor. Every Black family I knew had four magazines on their coffee table: *Ebony, Jet, Essence,* and *Black Enterprise.* I knew I had arrived when my grandmother Ozelia called and said in her southern creole accent, "Ooh, baby, you made Grandma and your family so proud."

Urbanworld Films was located in the new 550 Digital Media Ventures accelerator offices, directly across the street from the Sony building. We shared the space with other early-stage start-ups they had invested in. The offices were tricked out with an open-air floor plan, no walls, PlayStation consoles, and a fully stocked kitchen. The idea was to give a young start-up a place to focus on growing its business without needing to worry about office space and rent. It was a great setup. We had space to do our business in a very chill, relaxed atmosphere.

Things moved quickly. We started to purchase films and build out our technology. We were running the business on two parallel tracks: the theatrical and the dot-com. On urbanworld .com, we were doing deals with filmmakers with short films.

The short format worked better due to the low performance of the bandwidth. We had a large library of short-form urban and hip-hop content from Roc-A-Fella Records, Jay-Z, and more. The big streaming service that everyone was using at the time was Akamai.

Streaming business models had not formed yet. For the most part, you wanted to drive up traffic and then hope to monetize via advertising later. The experience was so bad and inconsistent. We were very early to the party, but we all still chased this streaming utopia that would come.

Within six months we had four feature films nearly ready for theatrical release: *The Visit*, starring Billy Dee Williams and Hill Harper; *King of the Jungle*, starring John Leguizamo and Rosie Perez; an urban comedy called *For Da Love of Money*, starring Pierre Edwards; and a film called *Punks*, which was about a Sister Sledge drag queen cover group. In addition to these titles, we had seventeen more in the pipeline. Everything was incredible!

CHAPTER 10

OUTSIDER'S ADVANTAGE

JUGGLING THE FESTIVAL and the dot-com business kept me extremely busy, but life was good. I was doing what I loved, showcasing programming that represented a broad lens of diversity across stories, characters, themes, and cultures. Plus, I was dating an incredible woman. I had not seen Marianne since that day in the elevator until we bumped into each other in 1997 at a Christmas party thrown by our mutual friend Jimmy. I told her about what I was doing with Urbanworld and invited her to our next festival. Well, not only did she take me up on my invitation, she became a volunteer, acting as the overall theater manager. She ran the screenings like a well-oiled machine. We were still just colleagues, but she was a great addition to the team.

In the summer of 2000, I was able to get four tickets to Shakespeare in the Park at the Delacorte Theater. It was my first time going, and I asked if anyone in the office wanted to go with me. Several people said they would attend, but Marianne was the only one who actually showed up, and in the end, it was just the two of us. The show was amazing, and it was a lovely night to be out in Central Park. Later in the week, Marianne asked if I wanted to go see a Luc Besson film, *The Big Blue*, that was playing at the Quad on Thirteenth Street. Of course I said yes, and thus began our journey and life together that has been going strong ever since.

———

URBANWORLD FILMS WAS creating a buzz. We were starting to make a name for ourselves as a distributor focused on movies for the Black community. But we were more than a "Black" distributor; we were getting attention in the industry at large. I was featured on the cover of the *Hollywood Reporter*, and in my mind, I was starting to become recognized by the establishment. Maybe I finally wasn't an outsider anymore. The work was hard, but we were riding a new and different wave. Our first theatrical release was *The Visit*, which was nominated for several awards, including the Independent Spirit Awards. According to the *New York Times*, we should have been nominated for an Oscar. Not too bad for our first release.

As successful as we were, it was still a hard business financially. We weren't producing films; our business model was what's known as "catch and release"—we acquired films for distribution. But the issue with catch and release is you operate on a LIFO system: last money in, first money out. This meant we put up finishing funds and marketing costs. Once the film started making money, we would recoup our money first, then split the additional revenue with producers. The finances for the theatrical business were very challenging, and very few movies made money. As a distributor, once you have paid to finish and release the film you only receive 50 percent of the ticket sales, and you get paid after sixty to ninety days. The margins were very thin. You then tried to make your profit from cable deals with HBO, Showtime, or Cinemax and DVD sales.

However, this did mean that in addition to running the business, I had to constantly raise more and more money to stay ahead of the grinder, eating up cash while we waited for revenues to come in. Sometimes it could take as long as eighteen months to recoup our costs. So I was always chasing investment dollars to keep the company running. When I would meet with potential investors, I'd give a big presentation complete with a PowerPoint slideshow, and I'd usually take the day before to stay home so I could tweak the deck and perfect my pitch. When I walked into that boardroom, I needed to be well prepared and on point.

I had a big presentation scheduled for September 12, 2001, with a large firm that was located at 2 World Trade Center. I was more nervous than usual about this meeting. There was the potential for big money, which would provide a nice cushion for us. As was my practice, I planned on spending September 11 preparing my pitch. I started the day with my daily run along the Hudson River. I was now living in Battery Park, an area located at the southern tip of Manhattan, and running along the river on a beautiful late-summer morning was just the thing I needed to begin my day with a clear head.

I got back to my apartment at about 8:30 a.m. Standing in the bathroom, I heard a plane flying overhead. This wasn't unusual; I lived in the penthouse—on the twenty-first floor of my building—and I would always hear planes flying by. However, this one sounded very low, and instead of the sound of a plane gliding toward the final approach, it seemed like the pilot thrust the engines to full power. Moments later there was deep boom and my building shook, causing cabinet doors to open and things to fall out. The lights dimmed, faded, then returned.

It had to be an explosion. I ran to the window and saw people holding their faces and pointing up to the sky.

An announcement came over the building loudspeakers: "Ladies and gentlemen, there appears to have been some type of explosion in the area. We are currently investigating." People were beginning to gather in the hall. I took the elevator down and ran out of the building, trying to figure out what was going on. People were screaming, "Oh my God!" I looked up and saw a plane sticking out of one of the Twin Towers. I prayed for those poor people. We all discussed how that plane must have somehow lost control, but it still sat with me that the engine's thrusting didn't make sense. The crowd was starting to disperse as some people went on their way, but then a second plane made its way south down the Hudson. It flew out over the Statue of Liberty and began banking to make a left turn. We figured it was going to fly over the tower and report findings. Then the scene that is burned into the minds of all Americans happened next. The second plane flew into the second tower. This was insane. My mind couldn't understand what was happening. *This can't be real.*

I had left my cell phone in my apartment, and I had to call Marianne. I needed to hear her voice and make sure she was okay; I needed to talk to her to try to make sense of this all. I made my way back upstairs and tried to call her, but the phone lines were down. I just kept getting a busy signal.

I went outside again, and the fires in both towers were increasing. The police had arrived, and they were trying to clear the crowd. They turned the lawn outside our building into a heliport. One of the emergency helicopters that had just been hovering above the towers landed on the lawn. I will never forget watching one of the firefighters exit the helicopter, fall to his knees, and begin smashing his helmet into the ground. We learned later that the doors at the top of the towers were locked, and there was no way to airlift people to safety. He realized the series of events that would, unfortunately, play out.

As I gazed back up to the towers, everything was starting to happen in slow motion. I couldn't fully comprehend what was going on. Nothing about this made any sense. The scenes that played out before my eyes are the ones many of you have seen on the news or in documentaries about September 11. The horror is nothing I could capture here in words.

I went back into the building and continued to try to reach Marianne but had no luck. Then we lost power. And then the unimaginable happened: the south tower collapsed. There was a rumbling, like a violent earthquake that seemed to last forever. Outside my window it seemed like day became night as a cloud of dust and smoke covered everything. Not long after, the north tower fell.

Even though I've relived those moments countless times in nightmares that I have had since then, I don't think I could accurately describe the events of that day. I do know that I went back downstairs to see if I could somehow help or do something. I tried to make my way toward where the towers once stood, but police officers were telling people to leave the area, that it was not safe. There were concerns that other buildings would start to blow up due to ruptured gas mains. The air tasted like metal, and my eyes burned. I made the decision to make my way to Marianne's apartment in the West Village. I walked along the Hudson River up the West Side Highway. Every once in a while, I would stop and turn around. The towers weren't there. How was it that they were not there?

There were only a few cars on the streets—mostly emergency rescue vehicles. At the intersection of Houston and West Side Highway two cars nearly crashed; one was heading west on

Houston and the other south on the West Side Highway. The cars came to screeching halts and both drivers leaped out. Harsh words were exchanged, and I just knew these two men—one Black, one white—were going to come to blows.

Then one of the men said, "I am on the job."

The other man said, "Sorry, brother, so am I."

They were both officers trying to get to the site to do what they could. The men hugged. A woman near me watching the whole thing started to weep. I swallowed hard trying to force down the lump in my throat. At that very moment, we could see that we were standing at the beginning of a new New York, a different America, a different world.

Since September 11, 2001, I am so grateful to be alive. That day clarified for me that you have to live every day as if it is your last, because one day it will be. September 11 taught me that this life is finite and there is no reason to hold back and wait for things to be right to live. To fight. To love. We have to do these things now. It doesn't matter what you have or don't have. It's so important to take your shot. If I were ever to be in a situation that I was not able to get out of, I did not want a life of regret for things I wish I had done. I made up my mind at that moment: I would honor the first responders, the firefighters, the officers, the men and women who lost their lives on that day by doing all I could to live my life to the fullest.

I realized what was important to me. One of those things was Marianne. We had talked about marriage before, but now I knew without a doubt that I wanted to spend the rest of my life with her. I proposed, and on December 31, 2001, we were married in an intimate ceremony. Life had become simple. Stop focusing on success and status. Focus on happiness and helping others. Build things that you're proud of, not things that you think will make you rich.

None of this stopped the reality that I still had to raise money for the company. We were quickly running out of cash, and many people were depending on me. I needed to keep moving. Unfortunately, it was impossible to raise money. I couldn't even get meetings. No one wanted to talk about business and sponsorship, and when I did get a meeting, everyone was just checked out. We were all acting like we were back to normal, but none of us were.

Bills were starting to pile up. I started having to let members of our staff go. Soon, there was no one left. I fought to save the distribution company by myself for a couple more years.

One day I walked into the lobby of my office building and a guy in a blazer said, "Are you Stacy Spikes?"

When I said that I was, he said, "Boy, you are hard to find. I have some paperwork for you." He was serving me papers from creditors. When we were no longer able to pay our bills, the vendors charged the remaining balance onto our corporate cards that were in my name. At the end of the day, the company was over $1 million in debt, and more than $250,000 of it rolled over on me personally. I went into my office and just cried. I had never fallen so far into debt. I didn't know where to turn.

Each day I went to the office alone. I felt like I was losing my mind. I grew to know the dark night of the soul that many founders experience in the face of failure; I became acquainted with that voice of despair that we all too often hear, for most founders experience failure before they taste success. But what I have learned is that the first failure is the most bitter, and the failures that follow—and in most cases, there will be more than one—sting a bit less. We hear the stories about the twenty-year-old founder who builds the billion-dollar company in his parents' basement. That makes for a good headline, but it's not the norm. The average successful founder is in his or her forties and has had two failed companies prior to success.

I've also learned that there really is no such thing as failure; it's all just learning. It's only a failure if you don't make room in your life to be able to learn. Most entrepreneurs I know are ten years ahead of the curve. They are building what is to come, not what is, and there is no way to accomplish that without trial and error. Fall down seven times, get up eight. Be teachable. Allow room to fall and get up and do it differently and better. I have become friends with learning, and once I was able to do that, being an entrepreneur wasn't so bad.

It also helps to have a couple of loving, experienced mentors in your life. They will save you when that voice in your head is trying to keep you down. They will guide you, support you, and help you not take yourself too seriously. I also love reading great literature; inspiring words have kept me going through tough times. Here are three of my favorite pieces.

"If"

RUDYARD KIPLING

If you can keep your head when all about you
    Are losing theirs and blaming it on you,
If you can trust yourself when all men doubt you,
    But make allowance for their doubting too;

If you can wait and not be tired by waiting,
    Or being lied about, don't deal in lies,
Or being hated, don't give way to hating,
    And yet don't look too good, nor talk too wise:

If you can dream—and not make dreams your master;
    If you can think—and not make thoughts your aim,
If you can meet with Triumph and Disaster
    And treat those two impostors just the same;

If you can bear to hear the truth you've spoken
  Twisted by knaves to make a trap for fools,
Or watch the things you gave your life to, broken,
  And stoop and build 'em up with worn-out tools:

If you can make one heap of all your winnings
  And risk it on one turn of pitch-and-toss,
And lose, and start again at your beginnings
  And never breathe a word about your loss;

If you can force your heart and nerve and sinew
  To serve your turn long after they are gone,
And so hold on when there is nothing in you
  Except the Will which says to them: "Hold on!"

If you can talk with crowds and keep your virtue,
  Or walk with Kings—nor lose the common touch,
If neither foes nor loving friends can hurt you,
  If all men count with you, but none too much;

If you can fill the unforgiving minute
  With sixty seconds' worth of distance run,
Yours is the Earth and everything that's in it,
  And—which is more—you'll be a Man, my son!

"The Man in the Arena"
THEODORE ROOSEVELT

It is not the critic who counts; not the man who points out how the strong man stumbles, or where the doer of deeds could have done them better. The credit belongs to the man who is actually in the arena, whose face is marred by dust and sweat and blood; who strives valiantly; who errs, who comes short again and again because there is no effort without error and shortcoming; but who does actually strive to do the deeds; who knows great enthusiasms, the great devotions; who spends himself in a worthy cause; who at the best knows in the end the triumph of high achievement, and who at the worst, if he fails, at least fails while daring greatly, so that his place shall never be with those cold and timid souls who neither know victory nor defeat.

"Invictus"
WILLIAM ERNEST HENLEY

Out of the night that covers me,
    Black as the pit from pole to pole,
I thank whatever gods may be
    For my unconquerable soul.

In the fell clutch of circumstance
    I have not winced nor cried aloud.
Under the bludgeonings of chance
    My head is bloody but unbowed.

Beyond this place of wrath and tears
    Looms but the Horror of the shade,
And yet the menace of the years
    Finds and shall find me unafraid.

It matters not how strait the gate,
    How charged with punishments the scroll,
I am the master of my fate,
    I am the captain of my soul.

I have seen the entrepreneurial life devour some people. The best advice I can offer after years in this game is:

- *You have to be willing to build things wrong in order to learn how to build them right.*

- *Raise your hand when you need help, and don't be too proud to lean on friends when necessary.*

- *Don't try to handle the pressure alone.*

- *And if it gets too dark, do not be afraid to get professional help. So often our society doesn't make room for that, but get the help you need and fight another day.*

Luckily, I took my own advice after being served with collection papers, and after getting some good counsel from close friends, I knew I could come back from this setback. I grabbed all the notices that I had been served and started making my appearances at the courthouse. I was in deep financial distress, but I wasn't going to run from my responsibilities. I showed up for all my court appearances in my best suit with all my paperwork in hand. I told the judge in each case that these debts were mine and that I would pay them off. Sometimes I was paying as little as $25 per month on thousands of dollars' worth of debt. It was so humbling. Some people advised me to just file for bankruptcy, but something didn't seem right about that. I worked and paid my debts. There was a small satisfaction paying off that money each month. It took me ten years to pay off those debts, but I eventually did it, and boy, did that feel good. In the years since, the universe started to send me other entrepreneurs who had hit bottom and needed help. It was my pleasure to guide them. I showed them how to go down to the courthouse, how to file paperwork and reply to the summonses, how to deal with aggressive collectors. I reassured them they would get through their times of trouble. They all did.

CHAPTER 11

"WHAT IF . . ." MOVIEPASS

URBANWORLD FILMS COULDN'T be saved, but I could now give my full attention to the festival. We had a very reliable and consistent track record of being able to draw star power and world premieres, and getting sponsorship was much easier. Heading into the 2003 festival, we had two new major sponsors. Kay Madati, who was the multicultural marketing manager for BMW North America at the time, brought us an opportunity with BMW Films. BMW produced a series of branded short films directed by popular filmmakers from around the world and starring Clive Owen as a driver. The shorts—each about ten minutes long—featured international celebrities and the latest BMW automobiles. As part of our sponsorship agreement, we would run one of the short films before each screening at the festival. The shorts we were going to run featured James Brown, Madonna, Don Cheadle, and Dakota Fanning. This idea of long-form branded content was groundbreaking, visionary, and way before its time. We would also have eight new BMW 325is parked in front of the theater with drivers who could take festival attendees for a free test drive. The drivers would also chauffeur VIP guests to and from the airport.

The other new sponsor was the Swiss watchmaker Swatch. They had agreed to sponsor not only the festival but our awards ceremony as well. We had decided to do the award ceremony at the Frederick Loewe Theatre at Hunter College on Sixty-Eighth Street. The Frederick Loewe Theatre was a classic performance theater with a blond mahogany stage and tall red curtains. It was the perfect venue.

The team at Swatch was so kind. I met Nick Hayek Jr., the CEO, at their US headquarters in Weehawken, New Jersey, and was shown how the watches were made by master craftsmen working in glass rooms. After the tour of their operations, they gave me four magnificent watches to wear on the red carpet. I was honored.

The awards ceremony was scheduled for Saturday afternoon, but by Tuesday we were already getting reports that Hurricane Isabel was coming up the coast and was scheduled to make landfall in New York City the day of the awards ceremony. We started getting cancellations and were worried that the theater would be half-empty, so we switched the venue to the much smaller movie theater where we premiered the films. Folks coming from out of town were naturally concerned about flying in for the event. Cedric the Entertainer was slated to MC the ceremony, but he and everyone coming from the West Coast canceled in a single day. The event was falling apart. I couldn't cancel on Swatch—they had a lot invested—so we did the best we could and hoped it would be okay.

On Saturday, the day of the ceremony, there was still confusion and people were showing up at the original Sixty-Eighth Street venue even though we had informed everyone that we had changed locations. We had someone posted at the

Frederick Loewe Theatre to redirect people, but they weren't showing up at the new location; maybe they just got frustrated and went home. And to make the whole thing worse, the hurricane shifted course, turning out to sea, and it ended up being a beautiful day. We were in a two-hundred-person auditorium and maybe thirty people showed up. I even had the staff come into the theater to add some additional bodies. It was bad.

Before the actual ceremony started, I was to be presented with an honorary key to the city. Just as the city official was giving it to me, I saw the Swatch team arrive. They filed in and surveyed the empty room from the back of the theater. I tried to keep a smile plastered on my face as I accepted the key, but I focused on the back of the house. I couldn't make out what they were saying, but there was a lot of hand-waving and angry faces. I felt terrible.

The following Monday, I got on the ferry and went back to the Swatch headquarters. I wanted to make amends for the dismal event, return the watches they had given me, and offer them the same level of sponsorship completely free for the following year. I told the receptionist why I was there, and she went into the CEO's glass office, where there was a lot of yelling and pointing in my general direction.

The receptionist relayed the message that the CEO was very upset, and that he said I should leave before he called the police to have me escorted out of the building. She looked very uncomfortable and embarrassed, but I knew she was just doing her job. I handed her the watches and said thank you and left. I felt so low that I went home and sulked for about a week.

No matter how confident you may be, sometimes you have setbacks. And it hurts to fail. At times like these, when I am at my lowest point, I find myself arguing with the critic in my head, who likes to declare that my career is over. You know that voice. *You're a loser. You always have been a loser.* It can be quite convincing. But over the years, I have developed a process for dealing with disappointments. First, I do my best to get away from everyone and sit in silence. I might even go away for a day or two. I let myself feel the full weight of my disappointment over things not turning out how I wished. Once I have bottomed out on that, I start to look at what I can learn from the situation. I learn what I did wrong and what I can do better next time. I try to be gentle with myself and remember the only people who never fail are the ones who never try. I like to write notes on the situation and analyze it like a scientist would—just the facts, not distorted by emotion. How could I have better promoted the event? How could I have better communicated to the attendees the change of venue? How could I have better communicated with my sponsor, to let them know what was going on? They may have been able to help. Should I have canceled the event? I run through alternative models in my mind, and once I feel I have looked at it from all sides, I might seek additional feedback from my team.

I remember that every situation is about learning. And when I look at it all as learning, I realize I can only become better for next time. Truthfully, the best learning experiences are often the most painful ones. The ones where you say to yourself, *I never want to go through that pain ever again.* It's taken me a long time to get to this point where I can view my failures as experiments that didn't work out. Having this perspective helps me to move forward in the right direction. I wish I'd had this point of view so much earlier in my journey. I took every success or failure so personally. But I guess those experiences were lessons too.

As demoralized as I was, I had no choice but to get back up and keep going. My family depended on me, my employees depended on me, and filmmakers depended on me to give them a platform. So the show had to go on, and it wasn't long before we started planning the 2004 festival.

The Urbanworld publicist at the time was Ava DuVernay. Ava was amazing. In this business, the most powerful player on your team when it comes to getting your premieres is your publicist. They are the ones with the studio relationships and the ones the studio trusts. In our early years, we used the Jackie Bazan Agency, which was run by Jackie Bazan-Ross and her partner, Evelyn Santana. Jackie was Spike Lee's publicist back in the day. After Jackie, we started working with Ava, who was daring and imaginative.

She called me one day and said she had a crazy idea. Now, Ava never thought small, so if she thought it was crazy, it must be a doozy. She told me she thought she could get *Collateral*, the new Michael Mann film starring Jamie Foxx, Jada Pinkett Smith, and Tom Cruise for the festival, and she could try to get Tom to attend. She conceded that it was a long shot, but it was worth a try. Ava said she would position it for Tom as the biggest movie premiere in Harlem history. We would shut down an entire city block and invite thousands of fans. Ava had it all worked out in her head and explained the grand design. We already had MTV and BET as sponsors, and she would partner with them to make this an over-the-top event. She had a few preliminary conversations with them, and things were looking good. I reached out to Swatch again because I wanted to make good on the disaster from the year before and felt like something amazing was coming together. They declined and didn't want anything to do with us.

We first got commitments from Jada and Jamie that they would attend. Tom was shooting *Mission: Impossible III* in Europe, and they were trying to figure out the logistics. MTV agreed to do an entire week in which *Collateral* would take over the channel. Promotion of the movie took place across all shows. At the start of each show, *Collateral* was talked about in the lead-in and some footage from the movie was shown. Then at the first commercial break, the commercial for the movie would run. There were contests and trivia done with the live audiences. In the movie, Jamie Foxx's character is a taxi driver, so MTV set up a show segment where Jamie would drive around in a taxi and pick up unsuspecting passengers. The video footage capturing their surprise when they finally realized who was driving is hysterical. Jamie taped several shows for MTV and BET that were going to air that weekend. We were doing the world premiere just days before the film opened internationally, and we scheduled an after-party immediately following, hosted by MTV, in the building next door to the theater.

Finally, just about two weeks out, Ava received the call confirming that Tom Cruise was going to be able to attend.

The morning of the premiere, the entire street behind the Magic Johnson theater at 124th Street was closed off and covered from curb to curb with a magenta carpet. Fan barricades and bleachers were installed along the sidewalks, with giant movie posters adorning the buildings. As we got closer to showtime, helicopters circled overhead, and the building and all areas around it were searched by bomb-sniffing dogs. Heavily armed security details coordinated with our team and stationed themselves in and around the theater and party venue. Trash cans were checked and then relocated. No stone was left unturned; with so much star power, we needed to have ultra-tight security.

Just as guests started to arrive, the air-conditioning system in the theater went down. The team jumped into action, getting someone on-site immediately to repair it. Crisis averted. Then Michael Mann announced he wanted to have the ability to control the movie's volume from his seat; the sound was still being mixed and he wanted to make sure the volume was right. Again, the team took care of things. Crisis averted.

The entire city block was packed with screaming fans as the stars began to arrive, first Jamie, then Jada, and finally Tom. Their professionalism was on another level. They walked the carpet and took photos and shook hands with everyone, treating each person as if they were a friend they had not seen for a while. I was very impressed.

Once everyone made it into the theater, Ava introduced me to the cast.

Tom shook my hand and said, "This is an amazing festival that you all have built. Thank you for having us."

I assured him the pleasure was ours and thanked them all for coming.

Ava and I escorted Tom, Jada, and Jamie to the stage, and Michael Mann introduced the cast. Then, after he made some brief remarks, the lights went down and the ride began.

The movie got a great reception. The after-party next door was packed, and the music was jumpin'. Doug E. Fresh was on the mic. At some point, Tom grabbed the microphone and gave a shoutout: "Yo . . . Harlem!" The place went wild. It was a good night.

I didn't know how we could top the *Collateral* premiere. How could we possibly grow the festival or the caliber of movies we were screening when we were already showing blockbusters and hosting A-list celebs? But I was always looking for new ways to expand the festival. I think that as an entrepreneur, your work is never done. You are constantly striving to make sure your business or product evolves and stays relevant to what is going on in the world around you. Change or die. I share the same philosophy as Sam Walton, the founder of Walmart and Sam's Club. He believed that there was no magic to success; it was merely a constant process of trial and error, over and over, and not being afraid to take risks. The question was, what should I try next?

Netflix was a young business and considered by many in the industry to be a joke. It was a subscription-based service that allowed customers unlimited access to movies for a monthly fee, but with a Blockbuster video store on every corner, how could a mail-order video subscription service ever succeed? However, the secret weapon was the subscription. The entertainment industry was constantly in the business of acquiring a customer over and over again. The studios and the video store had to lure customers in with advertising, promotions, and other incentives. But with a subscription, Netflix had a relationship with their customers. And it's easier and cheaper to keep a customer than to acquire one.

One night, I said to Marianne, "What if we made a Netflix for the movie theater industry? It's ripe for that kind of disruption." Marianne smiled and humored me. She was used to my crazy ideas. But here was my thinking: On average, the movie industry spent $7 to $10 to acquire a customer to see a movie. And when a ticket is purchased, half of that revenue is split with the theater. Most of the time, the theatrical window was breakeven, and all the profit had to be made downstream. If, however, there was a base audience of subscribers, you could eliminate the heavy, recurring acquisition costs and pull in a higher profit.

My initial thought was we could use this model to help get some of the films from the festival distributed. We would take the regular attendees of the festival, create a subscriber base, and that would fund at least one release in theaters every month, and ensure more films would get seen. The monthly membership could be equivalent to the cost of four visits to Starbucks: $20–$30.

I started to float the idea to some of the industry vets I

respected. I put together a deck and called the program Movies Unlimited. One of the first people I approached was Jack Foley. I invited him to lunch and talked over the idea. He loved it and said we should discuss it with Travis Reid. Travis was still CEO of Loews Cinema at the time, and he loved the idea so much that he granted me permission to run a test inside the Loews ticketing system. He told me that just a year earlier, AMC had tested a similar concept in one market and had gotten great results, but rumor had it that the program was discontinued due to some disagreement with studios about how the money would be counted. (I was later able to speak with one of the people who ran the AMC trial, and he confirmed that the financials actually did work.)

With Travis's go-ahead, I needed to figure out how to make it work. Fandango and MovieTickets.com controlled the ticketing landscape, but purchasing tickets on those platforms took about five minutes. Our goal was to streamline the process and make it possible for a subscriber to be able to purchase a ticket on our platform in less than sixty seconds.

The iPhone and mobile apps were still a few years away, so we did the transaction through SMS protocol. This was the user flow for the transaction:

Step 1: Customer types in movie and zip code.
Computer generates the four nearest theater locations.

Step 2: Customer picks a theater.
Computer lists showtimes.

Step 3: Customer selects showtime.
Computer confirms movie time and ticket.

Step 4:   Customer confirms transaction.
           Computer sends confirmation number.

Step 5:   Customer puts confirmation number in the
           kiosk at the theater to get tickets.

The first four steps took forty to sixty seconds and were smooth and easy. I worked with a company out of Australia called Soprano Design to build the back end. This was all coming together rather quickly. After we completed the code, we tested it inside the Loews system at their Thirty-Fourth Street location. I sat at a computer and made the first purchase. The team was able to confirm that the ticket had been removed from the inventory, and I was able to walk to the kiosk in the lobby and retrieve the ticket. End-to-end success.

Things were going smoothly until we hit our first bump. Travis called to let me know that Loews and AMC were merging and to continue with the subscription program I would have to take it up with Peter Brown, the CEO of AMC. Travis said he would make an intro.

Peter was based in Kansas City, Missouri, so I flew down and met with him. He had just completed the Loews acquisition and closed a major deal with IMAX, and I got the sense that he was meeting with me more as a favor to Travis than anything else. Peter explained that he believed IMAX was the future of the business and gave the theaters the ability to charge a higher price for a ticket. I tried to push my subscription idea, but it fell flat. He thanked me and wished me luck.

Travis still believed that what I was working on had merit and could help the industry, so he set up meetings for me with Regal and Cinemark, which were the other two top theater chains in the country. They, along with AMC/Loews, made up 50 percent of all ticket sales in the nation. They were kind, but my vision just wasn't resonating with any of them. The industry only seemed interested in the ability to upcharge the customer.

Richard Branson's Virgin Cinemas actually pioneered the all-you-can-eat theatrical subscription model in the UK in 1999, and soon similar programs were popping up across Europe. Yet I couldn't get any investors to back a similar product in the American market. I went to theater chains, studios, and investors all over the world for five years and could not gain interest or funding. I was sinking all of our extra money into this new company and not getting any traction. I just couldn't bring this idea to life.

———

THERE WAS A joyous event in *my* life, however. In 2006, Marianne and I were blessed with the birth of our daughter, Ellery. I had heard it said that you don't realize you can love something so much until you become a parent. I am here to confirm that it's true. Your life forever changes in ways you can't imagine. Family gave my life a different purpose and meaning. Business was important as a way of giving my family a quality life, but it was no longer my sole purpose. Marianne and Ellery were the center of all things. This was a shift from when the world was about my mission around a product. I used to live to work, but now I worked to live. I started to think about my legacy. Am I making the world a better place? Am I leaving it better than I found it? I don't think I would have been capable of seeing my work from that perspective before I had a family.

I continued to tread water on my subscription idea, but it was slow going. One Saturday, a dear friend of ours named Peter called and asked how the movie subscription idea was coming. He told me he'd had a conversation with his new employers, and they were interested in hearing more about it. He was very cryptic about who his new employers were, but it was the first good news on this front that I'd had in a long time, and I agreed to meet with these mysterious potential investors. The very next day, I took a taxi to the Central Park West address Peter had given me. I gave my name to the doorman, and he seemed to be expecting me. He directed me to the elevator, and as I rode up to the apartment, I questioned if I was crazy and if this was another wild-goose chase.

When the elevator doors opened, Peter was there to meet me. He wore a Cheshire cat grin and leaned in to whisper in my ear, "I'm working for Robert De Niro and his wife, Grace, and I told them about your project and they want to meet you."

Now I really thought this was all just a joke. De Niro? Sure.

Before I could respond, in walked a tall, beautiful woman who introduced herself as Grace Hightower. She was toweling off from a workout and apologized for her appearance. Her handshake was strong and confident. She was gracious and thanked me for coming to meet with them and asked if I needed anything. She said Bob would be down shortly. Moments later, Robert De Niro entered the room. He was very complimentary and anxious to hear more about my subscription concept.

I laid out my grand vision of the future and how I believed subscription could radically change our industry. They were an audience as engaged as any I had met with, and they deeply understood the business implications. Bob's questions showed his experience and depth of knowledge of the inner workings of the ticketing and advertising side of the business.

Leaving the meeting, I didn't know what to think. The whole situation was surreal in every sense of the word. What shocked me more was a few days later, Grace asked if my family and I would be willing to come and spend the day at their country house that coming weekend. Naturally, we accepted.

Their home was unpretentious and charming, and both Grace

and Bob were gracious hosts. Grace swept Ellery up in her arms and introduced us to some family members. Bob was sitting by himself by the pool when we arrived, and Grace escorted me over and left the two of us alone to talk. We talked very little about business; mostly we discussed life and family. Then Bob stood and said he had something he wanted to show me. He led me into the house and to a large room dominated by a full-size boxing ring. I thought Bob was going to tell me about his workout routine with his trainer, but instead he told me it was the original boxing ring from the movie *Raging Bull*. Bob told me how he saved up his money to buy it. I let my hand glide across the ropes and felt the smooth floor. As we leaned against the ropes, Bob talked about fighting for your dreams, believing in yourself, and how you must never give up. He reinforced the work ethic that I had heard from so many others. His words truly inspired me and have stayed with me to this day.

The following week, Grace asked me to lunch, where she let me know that she and Bob were interested in investing and becoming partners in the company. She personally wanted to be a fifty-fifty partner. We began the process of lawyers and paperwork. Over the next few months, there was a long slow volley back and forth. There were many different gatekeepers working on the De Niro/Hightower team. I had a meeting with one such gatekeeper who called me to the Tribeca offices for a meeting. We sat in his small, cramped office, where he said the Tribeca organization wanted to make me an offer. They were interested in buying both the Urbanworld Film Festival and the movie subscription company for one million dollars. I didn't have to think long about it. I politely said no, thank you. He said they had looked into my company and thought it was a fair offer. He also added that I could be employed and continue working for Urbanworld for at least the first six months of the new ownership. I thanked him again and left.

I immediately called Grace and said, "What was that?" She said she and Bob had no idea about such an offer being made. Bob asked me to personally come to his office, where he apologized to me and said he had no idea and he hoped it did not offend me. He and Grace still wished to do business with me. I let him know I was not offended and really appreciated his calling and meeting with me personally. I have to tell you, no matter what happened, the way Bob handled the situation spoke volumes to me and made me even more eager to partner with him. Since then, I have always tried to conduct myself with that level of direct personal accountability.

We got things back on track, but the paperwork was being held up for various reasons, and after a lot of back-and-forth, I just wasn't able to get the deal across the line. I had run up a legal tab too deep for me to chase any further. I sent Grace a heartfelt email letting her know that I needed to bow out and move on. I told her perhaps now was not the best time and thanked her and Bob.

I don't believe any encounters on your journey of building a business are ever wasted.

Perhaps the entire reason for that part of the journey was the time spent with Bob and the *Raging Bull* ring. His words echoed and have stuck with me. He gave me a gift that could not be bought. He gave me an unforgettable reminder of the importance of perseverance. I think the biggest thing that Robert De Niro taught me on that day was the importance of taking time and encouraging others. Pay your blessings forward. Sometimes a few kind words can keep a person going. It's important to know that although the path may be dark and lonely at times, if you just keep going, you will make it.

CHAPTER 12

DEVELOPERS AND DEADLINES

I T WOULD BE FOUR more years of ringing doorbells and being told no. All media innovation seemed to be happening at the device level. The focus was on computers and iPads and how movies could be played on devices instead of in theaters. I still believed the theatrical experience had room to expand, that moviegoing was a live event and not just a delivery system for films. At times I felt discouraged, but my resolve was restored just by sitting in a packed theater with other moviegoers.

There are times as a founder when you will find yourself challenging a system. The more innovative your product or service, the harder the pushback. But you need to persevere and remember that it's a marathon, not a sprint. Still, you also need to take a step back and look to see if there actually is a market for what you are attempting to introduce. You might be too early or too late. Or there might not be an actual need for your product.

In our case, we saw a delta between polls that said moviegoers preferred seeing movies in the theater and those that said they did not like the rising ticket prices. We believed we had a product that could fix that and decided to press on. I always try to periodically check my vision with my intended audience, and moviegoers regularly said they would like a subscription service to go to the movies. So I continued to forge ahead.

In 2010, I reached out to Guy Primus, who was COO of Overbrook, Will Smith's production company, at the time. I had met Guy at the Black Filmmaker Foundation's annual BFF Summit. Founded in 1978 by Warrington Hudlin, George Cunningham, and Alric Nembhard, BFF was originally started to help Black filmmakers, but eventually expanded to support all minorities in media and tech. I cannot overstate the impact the BFF Summit had on me and so many others in the industry. We would come together to celebrate one another's victories. We would learn from one another's challenges. And we would meet like-minded people in our industry who we could call on if we needed help. I can honestly say I owe many of my achievements to this group. It is so important to find a tribe of people who are striving to do something similar to what you are trying to achieve. Find other outsiders like yourself. Sharing knowledge, resources, and connections helps you all. Having a peer group to support and encourage you is a vital key to success.

So, through BFF I met Guy and pitched him on my subscription concept. He was very intrigued but felt he would not be able to get traction at Overbrook, since they were only focused on production at the time. He asked if I knew Hamet Watt from BFF. I was acquainted with Hamet, but we hadn't spent any significant time talking. Guy told me that Hamet was a venture capitalist in the tech space based in California, and he offered to introduce me to him.

From our first conversation, Hamet and I were finishing each other's sentences. We had so much in common and shared many similar views about the entertainment and tech industries.

Sometimes you meet someone and you just click. You know instinctively that this person can be trusted.

Hamet was excited about my idea, so he made some calls and came back and said he thought he could raise a million dollars in one month. If he could, would I be willing to be partners, fifty-fifty? I countered with sixty-forty, and he agreed. One month, one million dollars. He was confident he could do it, but I had met many people on this journey who made bold predictions, and none had succeeded. I liked Hamet, but it was an ambitious goal. So I just waited to see what he could do.

The first meeting he set up was with Mike Brown, who was at AOL Ventures in New York City. Hamet flew in for the meeting. He had such a confident and cool air about him—very LA—and he led the meeting with a let's-get-this-done attitude that I admired. Although I had been in many business meetings in my career, I was learning that the venture world had a language of its own, and Hamet and Mike spoke in this shorthand:

> MIKE: What's the concept?
>
> HAMET: Netflix for movie theaters.
>
> MIKE: Round? [*Translation: How developed is the business?*]
>
> HAMET: Seed. [*Translation: The earliest stage; ready to go from idea to prototype.*]
>
> MIKE: Valuation? [*Translation: How much is the business worth? This is usually based on a number of factors, including working capital, excess capital, revenue, debt, and projected profit, among others.*]
>
> HAMET: Four to five million dollars, pre-money. [*Translation: $4 to $5 million before any rounds of financing.*]

MIKE: Raise? [*Translation: How much are you
          trying to raise?*]

HAMET: One million dollars.

MIKE: We could do five hundred K.

HAMET: Okay, cool.

MIKE: Send me the paperwork.

HAMET: Done.

That was it. In thirty minutes we were halfway there. Mike Brown was our first check. It took another two or three weeks, but we then got another $500,000 commitment from Jon Callaghan at True Ventures, a venture capital firm based in Palo Alto, California, where Hamet was entrepreneur in residence (EIR).

Once we had our funding, we had to come up with a name for our new venture. We batted around a few names for the company but quickly settled on MoviePass—a pass for the movies. The consumer would pay one monthly fee and have a pass to go to a movie every day if they wanted to. We finished all the paperwork for incorporation and investments before Christmas 2010 and received funds toward the end of January 2011. We were off to the races.

Another skill that Hamet had was finding talent. He knew how to look at companies and use new tools like LinkedIn to find the best candidates to join our staff. Our first hire was Shane Bliemaster, who was at a start-up called Cherry Deals. Shane was originally from Detroit but was living and chasing the start-up dream in San Francisco. He liked our offer and moved to New York to join the MoviePass team. We quickly grew to about six people.

Part of the AOL investment included being part of their accelerator. Accelerators are support infrastructure for seed-level start-ups that include office space and services so that the company only has to focus on its product. It was very similar to the accelerator we were in at Sony. The AOL Ventures office was in Greenwich Village. It was a beautiful space with an open floor plan. There were rows of tables that sat ten people, and each company had its own table. This was the norm for accelerators. The offices tended to have the feel of a college student lounge with a kitchen, casual areas to relax, and a game room area. The AOL office was a bit more business-focused. We only had one pool table.

We moved quickly to develop the MoviePass app, with a June 27 launch in mind. Our goal was to have the consumer be able to complete their transaction in just three quick steps and to be able to do it all in the palm of their hand from their phone. I often have these visions in my dreams that result in déjà vu in the future. I'd had one a few years before the iPhone had been created, and I saw the features of the MoviePass app in my dream. It was amazing that within a few months I held that product in my hand.

We did a deal with MovieTickets.com, an online movie-ticketing website founded by AMC and Hollywood.com in 2000, to access their ticketing system. Before we signed the deal, we asked MovieTickets.com if we needed to present MoviePass to any of their theater clients, and they told us that our contract with them covered our ability to do ticketing at all the locations in their network. Our process with them was similar to what we had built with the Loews theater system, except the customer did not need to use SMS text; they would simply click the movie poster image of the movie they wanted to see and then select the theater and showtime. Once they confirmed their ticket, they would get a confirmation number. Shane and I planned a trip to San Francisco to test the technology for the first time at the Kabuki theater. We documented on video Shane pulling up the app, making the trans-action, and getting the tickets. All in all, the process took under sixty seconds! It was an exhilarating feeling to see this idea come to life. We knew we were going to use San Francisco as our launch market, so over the course of a week we went to theaters all over the area to test the system, and for the most part, it worked flaw-lessly. We were on track for our June 27 launch. We rented out an AMC theater in San Francisco and invited all the key Hollywood and tech press, as well as some interested investors. The plan was to show the technology to the press, screen the movie *Transformers*, and then be available for interviews.

On the night of the launch, Hamet and I stood on stage in matching red MoviePass shirts, did our presentation, and answered questions. The crowd was very supportive and enthu-siastic. Then the lights went down, and we started the screening. Some of the press started to hit within the first thirty minutes of the movie. *Wired* online posted "MoviePass launches Netflix for Movie Theaters." That headline stuck. Various versions of it ran worldwide, with more than eighty international articles on the first day.

Hamet and I were pulled out of the screening for a call from AMC. It was someone from their marketing team. It seems AMC was completely caught off guard by our announcement. They said they were a major shareholder in MovieTickets.com and that no one had discussed this with them. We confirmed that we had a signed contract with MovieTickets.com and had even paid them an advance against future earnings. We told the caller that we were only launching San Francisco as a beta market and assured them that we were sure we could all get on the phone the next day and clear things up.

We went back into the screening and all seemed to go off smoothly. We kind of just shook off the AMC call—we'd deal with that the next day—and focused on the event and the press rolling in. AMC hadn't made any demands of us; they seemed to just want to know what we were doing, since MovieTickets.com never made them aware of our deal.

I had an early-morning flight back to New York the next day. I woke up to the best news. Overnight we had nearly thirty thousand people trying to sign up for the service. We were on the cover of *Variety* and were featured in the business section of the *San Francisco Chronicle*. As my plane ascended, I felt blessed and immense gratitude that we'd had such a successful launch.

When I landed at JFK around 4:00 p.m., I turned on my phone and messages started loading. First the phone showed ten, then twenty, then thirty messages. They kept loading until I had more than fifty messages. I started listening to the messages, and it turned out the first messages were follow-up interview requests, but then about midway through my flight, AMC and Landmark Cinemas both released announcements saying they would not support MoviePass and that we had never gotten their permission to operate in their theaters. The remaining calls were from various press outlets asking for a reaction from me. I had planned to go home but instead went straight to the office to deal with the situation and do some damage control.

My first call was to Hamet, and the news wasn't good. MovieTickets.com said that AMC had forced them to cancel our contract. The press was having a field day with the story. It was being spun that we somehow mysteriously launched without the theaters' permission. On Thursday, *Variety* online announced the successful launch of MoviePass, and on Friday they reported our apparent demise, that we had been shut down by AMC.

There was a request for me to do a live television interview on MSNBC. I was anxious to set the story straight, so I accepted. The studio was in Rockefeller Center. I went to the greenroom to check in, and they informed me that the host was in Los Angeles and I would be doing the interview remotely. They led me to a small black room that contained a chair, a camera, and a monitor. They miked me up and ran a sound check. Then I was left alone in the room. A disembodied voice said we'd be going live in one minute. Before long, the monitor went on and I saw the host wrapping up a segment and then introducing me: "Next we will hear from the CEO of a start-up that tried to launch a new ticketing service without the permission of the movie theaters." I suddenly felt my throat go dry. The disembodied voice said, "Ready in five, four, three, two . . . segment."

The host started by talking about the concept behind Movie-Pass and the theaters' reaction before she finally addressed me. "So, Mr. Spikes, what were you thinking trying to go around the movie theaters to launch a ticketing service?"

Before I could get a full sentence out, she pounced on me again. She asked if it was just a case of my not knowing any better. Taken aback by this insult, I tried to sputter out a response, but then she went in for the attack again, questioning my business acumen and calling the entire thing a giant debacle. Before I could get another word out, she said we'd run out of time and thanked me for appearing on the show. The monitor went dark and the disembodied voice thanked me for my time as someone came in to remove the mic.

I left the studio absolutely devastated. I felt like I was blindsided and questioned whether I could have handled things differently. I had been working in the industry for years, and I think the thing that bothered me the most was framing the segment as if I were a novice who knew nothing about the industry, that I was an outsider. I was learning my early lessons about news cycles and PR spin the hard way. This felt like such a sucker punch. We had done everything by the book, and yet were being portrayed as rogue disruptors. I never watched the actual interview; it would have been too hard. I spent the next few days questioning everything. How did this happen? Was this all a bad idea? Did we screw up? What do we do now? A famous fighter once said everyone has a plan until they get hit in the mouth. Well, we just got hit.

When I went into the office on Monday, I was greeted with very long, worrisome faces from the staff. "What are we going to do now?" I was honest and said I didn't know. But I promised I would try to figure it out. As a founder, you will inevitably face disappointments and challenges. These moments are magnified when you have employees who depend on you and look to you for guidance. It's not necessarily about having all the answers, but it is about being honest with your team.

I called everyone into the conference room, and I spoke transparently. "We have six months of runway. We have to pivot and find a path forward. Our idea is sound, but we have to find a way around these large institutions that are very inflexible to new ideas. We have to be disruptive and change the way things are done. This is the way all great things are made. This setback is an opportunity for us. An opportunity for innovation and creation." I think I was talking as much to myself as I was to them. I realized I believed every word I said, and I hoped they did too.

Following the meeting, I took one of the whiteboards in the office and drew three circles. Top left, customer. Top right, theater. Bottom center, credit card. We knew credit cards were the easiest tool to complete a ticketing transaction, but we needed the ability to transfer funds to a customer instantly and allow them to purchase their ticket. To our knowledge, there wasn't such a system in place, and we needed a way to do it so that the theaters or ticketing platforms couldn't shut us down. I vowed that would never happen to us again. Seeing my perseverance seemed to shift the mood in the office. We may have hit a bump, but the wheels were still moving, and as the day wore on I could feel the momentum building.

We learned that there was a conference coming up in Las Vegas called the Prepaid Expo that focused on prepaid debit cards and other instruments of commerce. Geoff Kozma, who was the analytics whiz on our team, and I went. We typed up a piece of paper with four questions we would ask each vendor.

1. Do you have the technology to load funds to a debit card in real time?

2. Do you have the technology to use geo-location check-in to unlock funds?

3. Do you have the technology to make the funds exclusively available for one use (in this case, movie ticket purchases)?

4. Do you have the technology to enable us to retrieve funds if they are unused?

Geoff and I entered at one end of the cavernous conference hall and started going booth to booth with our four questions. We spent the whole day going up and down the aisles to every booth, and the answers over and over again were no. It seemed that the technology we needed just didn't exist. There were only credit cards, where the bank paid and you paid them back, or prepaid cards, where you put cash on the card in advance.

Slightly discouraged, Geoff and I decided to call it a day and regroup in the morning. As we were leaving, a man approached us. He introduced himself as Mark Tepper, the CEO of a credit card processing company called One to One. He said he had overheard us asking our questions and wondered if he could take a look at our list. I handed him our sheet of paper, and as he read, he just nodded his head and made a series of grunts, uh-huhs, and hmmms.

Handing the paper back, he said, "I think we might be able to help you, boys." He invited us to meet with him and his head of production, Nida Patel, in the lobby in about thirty minutes. Skeptical but intrigued, Geoff and I met them at the appointed time. Nida was a young woman in a hijab with piercing eyes. She got right down to business, going through each one of our questions and breaking down technically what was possible and how to achieve our needs. She had good news and bad news. The good news was that everything we wanted to do could be done. The bad news was that it didn't yet exist and we were going to have to be the ones to build it.

To me, this was great news. All I needed to know was that it could be done. If Mark and Nida could help us make it happen, then I was ready to do business with them. The following week, Geoff and I and some of our developers made a trip to Chicago to sit down with their One to One team. We hammered out all the details very quickly and got to work. Before long we had developed the app. Here's how it worked:

- The customer goes to the movie theater.
- They select the movie they want to see in-app.
- The back end operating system uses geolocation to confirm that the consumer is at the theater.
- Funds push to a MoviePass card.
- The customer uses the card to buy a ticket and goes to the movie.
- If the customer doesn't buy a ticket, the funds sweep off the card in twenty minutes.

All this would happen in milliseconds. It sounds relatively simple and straightforward, but there were so many nuances to it. For example, we needed to do the theater geolocation because on an earlier version we tested, college students were signing up for a single account but letting all their friends use it. When we added geolocation connected to the phone, it solved the problem. Many people would share their MoviePass card, but not many were keen on giving someone their phone. Another challenge we had was that there was no database that mapped the exact coordinates of the movie theaters. For example, if there was a theater just off the 495 freeway, the coordinates would be at the edge of the property line, which could be half a mile from the actual door of the theater. This may be inconsequential in a rural area, but in a city center you had to be accurate to within a few yards because in some locations (like Manhattan), theaters could be across the street from each other, and you'd never get an accurate reading.

We needed to test the user experience in real time. Ellery was six years old, and each weekend she would come with me, making rounds to different theaters to test the system. I would let her complete the transaction all by herself without saying a word. If a six-year-old could do it, we knew it was user-friendly. Ellery and I would also greet people in movie theater lobbies and tell them if they agreed to test the system, they could go to the movies for free. Ellery loved being part of the process, and having a six-year-old help do impromptu focus groups really increased participation. People trusted her and enjoyed interacting with her. We took copious notes, and I brought them back to the team every Monday. We were making good progress, but we were running out of time and cash. We tried to raise more funds, but most of the investors we went to were not interested. Usually, if you can show that you have a path forward, your initial investors will support you through the tough times, but AOL Ventures was going through some changes, and it didn't look like they would come through.

EVERYONE ON OUR small team was dedicated and worked tirelessly. In the midst of the vicissitudes of building a company, Ryan McManus, who is from Texas and has a quiet demeanor, joined MoviePass as an intern while we were in the AOL incubator. He started in customer service and quickly became a full-time hire and a strong force on the team. Ryan came to speak with me about wanting to grow within and become more valuable to the company. He said he wanted to become a developer. I told him it was a great idea and asked him to keep me posted. He committed himself to becoming an Android developer. He taught himself online and sought out other resources to learn everything he could. When a technical problem arose, Ryan would volunteer to look at it. He became more and more proficient in the various coding languages and found his area of expertise.

In time, Ryan became our lead Android developer. When we designed, we would often design in iOS and deploy Android later. Ryan made sure both apps would launch updates simultaneously.

Ryan was used to putting in long hours. I was glad to see he was on one of the local soccer teams and had a good work-life balance, which is so important for preventing burnout. One day he said he needed to leave a little early for an event and checked in to ask if I needed anything before he left. I was good but asked about the event. He had been volunteering his time with AllStarCode, an organization that teaches computer science to young men of color to ensure they have the tools they need to succeed in a technological world.

He reaches back and uses his skills to help other young men of color up the ladder. So many people don't do that. That humble leadership sets Ryan apart and makes me proud of him.

I decided to approach Jon Callaghan at True Ventures but didn't have high hopes.

Jon agreed to meet me on a Sunday night in their San

Francisco office, so I flew out on Saturday. The next evening, I drove over to the office but found it locked. I *was* a half hour early, but it was raining, and I wasn't sure what traffic would be like, so I wound up sitting in my rental car until Jon showed up. I learned he had just landed after a fourteen-hour flight and had come straight to meet me instead of going home to his family. Not the best circumstances to meet with someone to ask for money. Jon wasn't too chatty as he turned on the lights and led us to the conference room. He got right down to business.

"So, Stacy, what's going on?"

I quickly filled him in and told him that I thought we had come up with an incredible solution. "Over the past several months, the team has been hard at work and has achieved something both formidable and amazing."

Jon sat up in his chair, seemingly interested for the first time that night.

I continued, "For the first time, a customer can do a real-time funding load to a debit card based entirely on geolocation. We can lock the transaction down to a single location, even to a single kiosk." I slid a red MoviePass card across the table to him. I handed him my phone and let him walk through a transaction. He looked up and asked if it could be patented. I told him that patents had already been filed and were pending.

He leaned back in his chair and said, "Stacy, this is impressive. I like it. We'll invest an additional round. I will discuss this during our committee meeting tomorrow, but tell the team I said good work."

We had a lifeline, and we were back in the game.

———————

WE TARGETED October 2, 2012, for our launch date. We hired a new PR firm called LaunchSquad that specialized in

launching tech start-ups. The team was made up of Marissa
Arnold, Hela Sheth, and Gavin Skillman. They had a completely different strategy. We knew press like the *Hollywood
Reporter* and *Variety* would always side with the theaters, so we
needed to go to the tech press instead. We needed outlets that
supported trying new things, disruption, and innovation. We
were something new, and the establishment was uncomfortable with us. People were still smarting from our first launch
attempt. Shari Redstone, daughter of Sumner Redstone and heir
to the Viacom family business, was onstage at a movie industry
conference when she was asked about MoviePass. She said a
subscription model for the movie industry wasn't wise, but she
felt if the industry was going to have a subscription service it
should be done from within, not from outsiders. Funny being
referred to as an outsider of a business that you've been a part of
for most of your life. But this was nothing new for me. I have
been considered an outsider my entire life, whether it be for my
race, my industry, or my ideas. But if I was not an outsider, I
would not have some of the views that are critical to our success
in the market. In particular, we were building a company from
the consumers' perspective. We were neither theater nor studio.
We were just movie lovers.

As we neared the launch, Hamet and I debated whether we
should launch one market, like we had with San Francisco, or
go nationwide. I was adamant we needed to launch nationwide.
If we launched in a single market, it meant those local players
would have to react, but if we launched in all markets at once, it
was less likely they would be able to respond as before.

We settled on the full nation. Our footprint would be larger
than Fandango and MovieTickets.com combined. Our motto
was *Any movie, anytime, anywhere, for one low monthly fee.* Travis

was still very supportive. He reached out personally to the CEOs of the top three exhibitors—AMC, Regal, and Cinemark—and let them know what our intentions were and that I would be happy to speak with them directly. I also sent each of them, and the CEOs from all the other exhibitors we had built relationships with, an email inviting them to come to me with any questions or concerns.

I got a call from Josh Dickey, the *Variety* writer who had covered MoviePass in the past. Josh said that he heard we had a new product coming and offered us an opportunity to give him the exclusive. We passed. He said *Variety* had the knowledge and would run an article without us. We told him to go ahead. We knew there were no leaks on our technology.

The following day, on October 2, we dropped the announcement of the new product. We provided the information to *Tech-Crunch*, *Wired*, *Engadget*, and other tech press that had been supportive in the past, with the understanding that they would not release anything early. *Variety* picked up the story, and we were very surprised by the headline: "Third Time's the Charm for MoviePass?" Josh actually wrote us a glowing article and explained how we were reinventing moviegoing. The tech press framed us as underdogs fighting the movie industry. We were finally getting traction.

CHAPTER 13

DEFENDING THE CASTLE

THE RELAUNCH WAS a success. However, we discovered one area that could affect the business: escheatment laws. Escheatment is the idea of returning lost or unclaimed property. You see this with gift cards. Let's say you put $40 on a gift card and don't use it. The company must hold the value of the $40 on their books, and after a period of time, if it's unused, it is returned to the customer. If it is not returned, then Uncle Sam declares it as income and taxes the company.

The MoviePass model was more like a gym membership in that you are buying a block of time (one month) to use the service and at the end of each month the clock resets. So, there is not a rolling balance that the company has to keep on its books. This took some time to figure out with accountants, because each state has its own escheatment laws.

The launch also enabled us to learn a lot of information fast. I have always been enamored by data, and MoviePass was allowing us to have insight into moviegoers' behavior like never before. We could see migration routes, where people in certain communities that might not have had the best theaters would migrate to other areas. We saw how certain families would go to the movies in packs. We noticed a distinct pattern with individuals with long commutes. They often were the ones who went to the movies once per week on their way home while they waited for traffic to die down.

But here is the information that made MoviePass and its concept so powerful for the movie industry: MoviePass increased consumers' behavior by 100 percent. If a moviegoer went once per month, with MoviePass they increased to twice per month. If they went twice a month, they would increase to four times a month. Another powerful piece of data gave us a peek into the mind of the consumer. It seemed that for most subscribers, not having to pay each time they went to the movies increased their concession spend by 120 percent. When you combined the increase in attendance and concessions, our rough data showed that we increased the average consumer from $120 per year to nearly $400 in ticket and F&B (food and beverage spend). IMAX and 3D did not increase sales like this.

One of the concerns that the industry had was that we might be cannibalizing weekend ticket sales. In other words, they thought the subscription model was bringing down the average cost of the ticket and thereby reducing the profit that the theater would receive. This was false. However, what we found in the data was even more surprising. Looking at our data and posted box office sales, we could tell that with major releases like *Star Wars* or *Harry Potter*, moviegoers tended to purchase tickets well in advance on Fandango or MovieTickets.com to make sure they saw the film within the first day or two of release. MoviePass just didn't have the capability for advance purchases because it could only be used at the kiosk as a walk-up transaction. But when they went to see the movie the second or third time, they used their MoviePass. Now, instead of waiting for a movie to come out on a streaming service or video on demand, they went to see it again in theaters. Because we were only available for walk-up ticket purchases, we were using only remnant inventory and not cannibalizing the seating as feared. This was all lift and no drag, as we liked to say. The performance numbers were through the roof.

In October 2014, Hamet and I were able to spend some time with Gerry Lopez, the CEO of AMC, at the BFF Summit. Gerry helped us to understand the reaction that AMC had when we first launched. In short, they were not informed about the launching of the service and were caught off guard. Gerry was protective of AMC customers' experience and did not want a situation that could potentially negatively affect their visit. We found him to be smart, innovative, and very open-minded. He and his team were leading the industry when it came to enhancing the customer experience—updating their theaters with reclining seats, improved food and beverages, and wider aisles. Gerry wasn't afraid to shake things up in the industry. We shared all our findings with Gerry and asked that if we could prove lift on attendance, loyalty, and concessions, could we figure out a strategic partnership? We proposed to do a double-blind study run by an independent third party who would produce a white paper with the results. Gerry expressed the concern about cannibalization that we had heard before, but we assured him we had the data and believed the report would confirm that his fears were unfounded.

Gerry agreed and said he would give us a chance. He felt that if our data was right, MoviePass could only be a good thing for the industry and a great partnership for AMC. He put us in contact with Christina Sternberg, AMC's head of corporate strategy and communications. She was leading the charge to upgrade the theater experience. Christina is just one of those great people you can't help but love and appreciate.

She's no-nonsense but handles business with a smile and treats everyone with respect. We got the details of our deal hammered out pretty quickly with her. We agreed to use Mather Economics to conduct the study and to test in two markets: Denver and Boston. Boston would be an integrated market where the ticketing was direct and the consumer did not need to go online or to a kiosk. They would be able to select their seat right in the app (however, tickets would still only be available for the day of, not for advance ticketing). We wanted to see if direct API sales increased loyalty to AMC. The assumption was if a person had the choice to go to the theater and purchase a ticket or be able to do it directly in the app with AMC from home, they would choose AMC. The Denver market used the standard process.

We announced the joint test in the market to some raised eyebrows. Everyone was curious to see if the former rivals could be allies.

Although we were finally getting major traction in the industry, we were running very low on cash. We desperately needed to find a way to keep things going. Hamet had been doing an excellent job of finding us capital, but now the traction we were getting with AMC was driving the cost up. We needed to make it to the next ridge while we still could.

A man I will call Ben, one of the principals at a previous investor, had moved to a new shop and was willing to throw us a lifeline. I flew to California to have a meeting with him, but it seemed more like a formality, to show him respect. As usual, Hamet did most of the talking, and we were in and out of there in about forty-five minutes. Paperwork for a million-dollar bridge loan was being drafted and would be sent to us in a few days.

We redlined the first draft and quickly went back and forth. There was one sticking point that we couldn't get past: the ability for Ben to call the loan six months early at his discretion. Hamet and I debated what to do, but we were in dire straits; we had not been paying ourselves for months, and we were up against the wall. With no other prospects in sight, we reluctantly signed the deal.

You know exactly what I am about to say. Yes, Ben called the loan early. We were on the hook for $1 million and had no way to repay it. If we defaulted, he could put a lien on our assets and intellectual property, basically forcing us to sell the company to him.

We had a small window for repayment, and I was flying all over the country trying to meet with investors in an attempt to save the company. In the midst of this, in March 2015 I was invited to South by Southwest, the premier festival for leading innovators in the tech, film, and music industries. MoviePass had been selected for inclusion in their 15 Disrupt section, a group of the fifteen top disruptive companies in the world. It was a pretty big deal. At SXSW I ran into an old friend from my Miramax days, Ted Hope. Ted was a film producer with a fantastic track record who was now working at a start-up called Fandor, which was like a Netflix for independent and international films. I filled him in on what was happening with MoviePass, and he suggested I speak with his boss, Chris Kelly, who was the principal investor at Fandor. Ted emailed Chris to make the introductions, but I had to fly home the next day. Hamet was able to take the meeting, and Chris and I scheduled a call for the following week. Chis seemed interested in MoviePass, and we started to have weekly calls. We developed a good rapport, and Chris seemed sincerely interested and very engaged. But you just never know.

Meanwhile, Ben was becoming more aggressive as the

deadline approached. He called to say he would be coming to New York and wanted to sit down with me to discuss matters. A week or so later, we all met in our New York office. Ben jumped right in and started to tell me how things were going to go down now that he was going to be taking over the company. First, he said MoviePass would be moved to California and be run out of his office. Any staff who were willing to make the move had a chance to stay on, but if they weren't willing to relocate, they would be out. He had a new CEO lined up, a man by the name of Mitch Lowe, who had already accepted the job. And as for me, he would let me work for a few months to see how I performed and then he would decide if he would keep me or not. Anger doesn't begin to describe how I felt.

I stood up and said, "Thank you for coming, but you need to leave. You greatly underestimate me. You will have to pry this company from my cold, dead hands."

Ben just stared at me for a moment and then stood up and left. I didn't bother seeing him out.

I continued to fly all over the country chasing money, working the phones, picking up a few investors here and there, but it was not enough to stop Ben from coming. I realized that if he had Mitch agreeing to be the CEO, there were more inside players than I'd thought. Mitch was on the MoviePass advisory board, so they clearly had been colluding behind my back.

Another realization hit me like a slap in the face. I was having trouble making headway with investors but didn't know why. I was a successful entrepreneur. The entertainment projects I had shepherded had grossed more than three billion dollars in sales. I was named one of *Hollywood Reporter*'s thirty under thirty. I had built the world's largest minority film festival. And more than that, all the data from the relaunch was proof that MoviePass was a winner. And yet I wasn't raising the funds we needed. I was getting into the rooms, but I wasn't getting to yes. I was beginning to think that race must be a factor. There is a stereotype when it comes to successful tech entrepreneurs: they are young, white, went to an Ivy League school—or dropped out of one. I didn't fit that bill. In fact, in not one of my meetings in Silicon Valley or Silicon Alley, on Sand Hill Road or Boston Technology Corridor, did I ever see a single person of color in a decision-making position. Geoff would often travel with me to meetings, and he looked more the part than I did.

Once, we were sitting in a conference room waiting to meet with a venture capitalist, and when our host walked in, he went straight to Geoff, and said, "Stacy, it's such a pleasure to meet you."

Geoff pointed at me and said, "That's Stacy."

The rest of the meeting was awkward.

The harsh reality is that less than 3 percent of venture capital investments go to women and minorities. There is an invisible bias at work. Sure, no one is mean. No one calls you the N-word behind your back. It's more subtle than that. It's about perception. The perception that you are not as smart. You don't have resources. You are considered to be a higher risk. There's the belief that you won't know how to pivot. You may break under pressure. You don't look the part. You don't look like *them*. You have to be twice as smart, work twice as hard, and pay twice as much to get to the same place. Some of us entrepreneurs of a darker hue call this the "Black tax," that invisible burden that minorities know so well when it comes to trying to buy a home, get a promotion, and, yes, get financial backing for your business. This is getting better and slowly changing. Following the death of George Floyd, the level of diverse funds has increased. But entrepreneurship is hard no matter who you are, and if you are a woman or a minority, things are harder. I don't say this to be discouraging, but just to point out certain realities that are part of this process. There are investors out there who will believe in you, but you may have to walk farther to find them.

This was my reality, and time was running out. I was finding it harder and harder to sleep and eat. But I couldn't let Ben take my company away from me. I needed to find the strength to keep going. Growing up, I was taught—by my parents, my grandmother—to turn to scripture for guidance through difficult times. This might not be for everyone, but it has worked for me. The scriptures, at the end of a long, hard day, are like a soothing balm to my wounds.

"No weapon formed against me shall prosper."
(ISAIAH 54:17)

"Some trust in their war chariots and others in their horses, but we trust in the power of the Lord our God."
(PSALM 20:7)

In addition to getting deeper into scripture, I meditated to ground myself. I needed to have a clear mind, free of self-doubt and fear, in order to keep focused on the task at hand. I couldn't let my own negative thoughts sabotage my efforts. Just ten minutes each morning helped me start the day ready and determined to persevere. I also added more running. For years, early-morning runs had been the best way to prepare for important meetings and presentations, but I had read an article in the *Wall Street Journal* about people who ran a mile or more daily. Some maintained these running streaks for as long as forty years. Since reading that article, I committed to doing the same, and have not missed a single day of running since.

The deadline was closing in. I had about two weeks left before we would lose the company due to the inability to pay the loan back in full, plus interest. Day and night I made calls, chased leads, followed up on promises . . . and nothing. I continued to have my Thursday-morning calls with Chris, but I still didn't have a commitment from him. It was like a slow courtship, just feeling each other out but neither of us wanting to seem too eager. I was reluctant to tell him how close we were to defaulting; I didn't think it would help him feel confident in me as a businessman. Desperate, I finally just came out and asked Chris if he was interested in investing. He said he would be in New York the following week and we could discuss it in person. It turned out that the day we were to have our meeting was the exact day I was to sign over the company. Any hope I had for an eleventh-hour rescue was extinguished.

It was Wednesday morning, and I had not slept at all the night before. Life as I knew it was ending. I couldn't believe that I had fought so hard and had come so far just to lose MoviePass like this. Sadness, defeat, and rage commingled within me. Before I left for my lawyer's office, Marianne gave me a kiss and a tender hug.

"Honey, I am so proud of you and all that you have accomplished. You are a good man," she whispered in my ear.

The taxi made its way through the sleepy traffic as melancholia colored my vision. The city was different. Its streets didn't pulse with life and opportunity as they had even just the day before. Now it was a town whose mill had shut down and hope had moved away.

At the lawyer's office, I was escorted into the conference room by a kind receptionist who seemed to have a sense of the situation. "Sasha will be right with you," she said as she exited, pulling the frosted glass door closed behind her.

Shortly, Sasha entered, greeting me with a firm handshake

and a deep smile. In no mood for pleasantries, I cut straight to the point: "So, what are my options?"

Sasha had nothing to offer. He removed some documents from a folder and started outlining what would happen once I signed. I stood in front of the giant glass window looking out upon the dense metal and concrete landscape. I wasn't listening; my mind had drifted. My mind had the ability to leave a situation and go deep into itself. My second-grade teacher wanted to keep me back a year because she felt I was slow and prone to daydreaming. But this daydreaming was a form of focus and problem-solving that has served me greatly in life, the ability to be in full-battle situations outside but stay calm and still on the inside.

At that moment, the story of Moses on the run from Pharaoh was playing in my head.

I heard the dialogue that Moses was having with God. He went to him and said, "Pharaoh is behind me, and the sea is in front of me. Please help save us."

God's response is so interesting. He says to Moses, "Why are you crying to me? I gave you all the strength and power you need to get through this situation. You go and take your staff and part the sea yourself."

Moses is confused. *You gave me the power?* As Moses makes his way down, he raises his staff and strikes the sea, and it parts.

In the telling of that story, people often say God parted the sea. But I think it's talking about believing in your God-given talent to problem solve. The sea is the opportunity to invent and reimagine. Pharaoh is the catalyst for that change. The driver of the innovation.

I turned to Sasha. "I'm not signing it," I said. "I'm not sure what I'm going to do, but I have to do something. I'll call you later."

I left the building, and even outside, that biblical passage kept ringing in my head. *I've given you what you need; you part the sea.* Perhaps hope hadn't left this town yet.

I went to the office with a quick pace to my steps. "Good morning, everyone," I said when I entered. "Why so serious?"

They asked me if I had signed the documents.

I said, "No. We're not going down without a fight."

You'd swear someone had just burst into a funeral with news that the deceased was found alive. I asked them to think of all the scenarios they could to get us through the weekend. We were going to run out of money in forty-eight hours, and the entire system would collapse.

By now, Ben's lawyers knew I hadn't signed the documents and they were not happy. They informed Sasha that they were going to try to get a court injunction to prevent me from running the company off a cliff. They believed that I had somehow gone crazy and decided to let the company run out of money and damage the intellectual property to injure their investment. Interesting thought, but it couldn't be further from the truth.

Ben began blowing up my phone with calls and texts. *What are you doing? . . . You need to sign those documents. . . . You are in breach. . . . We will sue you.*

I had no time or inclination to respond. I had to meet Chris and Hamet at the Mercer Hotel for lunch. As I walked there, I realized that I was truly confident that we would find a way through this. *You part the sea* kept echoing in my head. I entered the Mercer and made my way to the main lobby, where I saw Hamet sitting. He had flown in from LA the night before for this meeting and we hadn't yet spoken. He had a look of fear, fight, and confusion in his eyes.

"Stacy, what did you do?" Evidently Ben had been trying to contact him too.

Before I could get into it, we saw Chris approaching. It was my first time meeting him in person. He was tall and had a Boy Scout's honest smile.

"Hey, fellas. Let's go have some lunch."

Once at our table, we exchanged pleasantries and then Chris said, "So, I read the loan docs on the plane, and it's got hair all over it."

Hamet and I nodded in agreement.

"I think you guys have a great company and huge potential, but this is a very bad deal."

Hamet started discussing terms and ways we could sweeten the deal to help get Chris across the line. Chris went on almost as if he were having a conversation with himself.

"The thing I don't like most about this is when bad people try to take advantage of good people in such a mean way. I just don't like that."

It sounded like Chris knew what was going on with Ben. I guess it wasn't such a big industry after all. Chris circled back around to the terms Hamet had laid out. We agreed on a discounted round. We then discussed the funds we needed in the short term.

Chris paused for a brief moment and then said, "Okay, let me send the terms to my attorney." He pulled out his laptop and started to type up a term sheet right there. He cc'd us on the note to the lawyer that basically said he would buy out the loan plus give us $1 million to get over the next few weeks, transferring $500,000 the next day, in time for the weekend.

After he sent this email, which took all of five minutes, he closed his laptop and said, "I'm looking forward to working with you, gentlemen. I think this company can change how people go to the movies forever."

I excused myself to go to the restroom. Did that really just happen? I looked in the mirror and grabbed my face, willing myself not to cry, but I couldn't fight the tears. Thankfully I was alone because I sobbed, saying over and over, "Thank you. Thank you."

Once composed, I returned to the table and our lunch meeting ended as casually as it began. I had to make my way over to a speaking engagement, and a few hours later, just before I was to go onstage, Chris's lawyer sent over the docs. I signed and returned them immediately. The next day, true to his word, Chris wired the funds. That was Thursday, and we wired those funds to our ticketing account with hours to spare so we would have funding through the weekend.

From lunch to my speaking event, I had little time to call Marianne, and when I tried, she didn't pick up. I didn't want to leave her some weird voice mail, so I decided to wait until I got home to tell her the news. When I walked through the door, she had a beautiful dinner set on the table. She asked, "How did it go, honey?"

I said, "You're not going to believe what I am about to tell you." She braced for some horrific war story of heartless capitalism, and instead she heard a story of human kindness. Her face registered her disbelief, so I pulled up Chris's email on my laptop. She smiled as tears welled in her eyes. Miracles do happen.

CHAPTER 14

WHEN THE WALLS COME TUMBLING DOWN

NOW THAT WE had dodged a major bullet, we had to continue with our mission to prove our math to the industry in the form of the Mather report. The process was that AMC and MoviePass would provide all their transactional data in the Denver and Boston markets over a six-month period. Mather would cross-reference and find matches between the MoviePass and the AMC customers and then go back in time and look for a behavioral lift in attendance and concession purchase behavior.

If the Mather report could prove that MoviePass increased ticket sales, it would pave a pathway to working with the industry as a whole.

The Boston market proved to be of interest very early on, because for the first time, we made it possible for users to use the app to select their seat and get their ticket all from home. To prevent fraud and people booking a ticket and not using it, we designed the system so that your ticket was held, but the confirmation number was not released until you checked in using your geo location once at the theater. The app would then show you your confirmation number so you could retrieve a paper ticket from the kiosk, or you could just show the ticket taker a QR code. If you booked a ticket and did not go to the movie, we would charge you back the price of the ticket as a no-show.

Amazingly, we saw a 30 to 40 percent lift in AMC theaters with electronic ticketing capability. This meant that our subscribers were choosing electronic ticketing at AMC over walk-up at other theaters. We called this "lift and shift." The lift was an overall increase in going to the movies. The shift was switching from one theater to another. We did not see any cannibalization of weekend tickets because we were still only offering tickets available the day of.

The relationship with Chris was going well. We also were forming a strong relationship with the AMC team. We flew to their headquarters in Kansas City a few times. On one occasion, I brought Chris with me so he could meet Gerry. They really hit it off, and we made plans for the AMC and MoviePass teams to get together at Chris's home sometime in the near future to explore our options going forward. Things could not be looking better.

The Mather report was finally publicly published after a year and a half. The overall lift came in at around 111 percent, month over month, with an average lifetime of twenty-four months. The report found that the average customer went to the movies 2.5 times per month. The average monthly subscription price was around $30 per month at the time. This was industry gold.

Gerry was very impressed with the results and agreed to make MoviePass available and integrated across the entire AMC system in the United States. If the trends we saw in the test market played out across the country, Gerry would make the introduction to the team at the Wanda Group, which owned AMC and was the largest cinema operator in China. One of the remarkable things about Gerry is that he did not want AMC to have any type of monopoly or exclusivity over MoviePass. He believed, as we did, that it was better that this technology remain equally available for all exhibitors.

Things couldn't be better . . . until everything started falling apart. I got a call from Gerry letting me know that he was leaving AMC to pursue a new opportunity. He told me to keep pushing MoviePass, that we were on to something big, and if he could be of assistance to let him know. Christina Sternberg departed weeks later. The entire MoviePass program was put on hold during AMC's CEO search.

Even with the publishing of the Mather report, we still were not getting engagement from Regal or Cinemark, but we did start to get traction with players like Marcus Theatres, Studio Movie Grill, B&B Theatres, and more.

Still, the overall feedback we received from the venture capital community was that if the major theaters weren't investing in MoviePass, why should they? Chris was financially carrying the company and began growing weary on our Thursday calls. He started to hint more and more that he wasn't going to be able to keep going.

In December 2015, AMC named Adam Aron as its new CEO. He was the former CEO of the Philadelphia 76ers. I began making regular calls to his office to schedule some time to discuss MoviePass. Finally, Hamet and I were able to have a call with him, and he said that, coming from the sports world, he believed in the power of subscriptions and talked about the importance of arena box seats and season ticket holders. Those were the cornerstone of the live sporting business. But he did not want the future of AMC to be in the hands of a "start-up," as he put it. He did add that he was interested in considering a white-label deal where AMC would brand the technology and have it available only in AMC theaters.

This was a no-go for me. This deal wouldn't have just been bad for MoviePass, it would be bad for the industry as a whole. The data showed that a subscription plan was beneficial to everyone. If MoviePass partnered exclusively with AMC, the other theater chains would inevitably create their own systems, and therein lay the problem. Having a universal system for customers makes adoption easier. Early on, if you tried to launch different ticketing platforms for each theater circuit, you would not be able to create uniformity, and this would slow down adoption. Also, we had to remember that the studios had a level of financial mistrust because when the theaters tried adopting a subscription model in the past, there was not a clear accounting regarding the subscription and what actual tickets were sold. Finally, in our system, we noticed moviegoers attended three different theaters throughout the year: two major theaters and one art house. We also saw that the art house theater was more heavily trafficked during Oscar season. Customers would have to get three subscriptions, and more than likely they would not do that. They would either get one and forgo the other theaters or not take on any subscription at all. Multiple systems would most likely drive down attendance.

I am not implying that MoviePass should have been the only option. I don't believe there needed or should have been a single theatrical subscription company. There should have been several. Competition is always good. And I understand the idea of wanting to create an advantage for AMC, but I felt Adam's offer was shortsighted. We had empirical data that showed we had what would create a boost for the overall industry and save studios on the cost of customer acquisition on third-party advertising platforms like TV and online.

Chris, Hamet, and I huddled to discuss our next moves. It seemed the only pathway forward if the big three exhibitors were not going to play was to try to ramp up with some of the mini majors we had already been speaking with.

––––––––––

EARLY IN 2016, Chris called me and said he was traveling and had a layover at Newark; he wanted to know if we could have breakfast. We met early on a Sunday at the airport. I braced myself for what was coming. He said he had made the decision that he wasn't able to go on with MoviePass, but he had an offer from Mitch Lowe—yes, the same Mitch Lowe from before. Chris told me he was not interested in forcing me out of the company, but he could only continue to support the company financially if Mitch was the CEO. He said he would understand if I didn't want the change, but if not, he was out.

I didn't know what I was expecting, but it wasn't that. I asked him if he really had a layover, or did he just fly out on the red-eye to have this talk with me, man-to-man, in person. He nodded briefly and said, "In person." I asked him if he had looked at any other CEO candidates. He said no. I told Chris on the spot that I was willing to support his idea given that he had not only rescued us in the past but he had also been supportive over the last two years and had invested a lot of money in us. Plus, I really appreciated his compassion and the human decency he showed by coming to deliver the news in person.

Chris arranged for the three of us—him, me, and Mitch—to meet in San Francisco to discuss transition and roles going forward. It was the summer of 2016. We were meeting at a WeWork, but at the last minute, Chris said he couldn't get away and would call in to the meeting, so it was just me and Mitch in the room. Chris made some opening remarks about how he was looking forward to the next chapter of MoviePass and was excited to see us working together. Then he jumped off the call, and Mitch and I went to work. It was mostly Mitch asking questions and me answering.

"I'm surprised you're staying with the company," Mitch commented.

"Why would I leave something I built?" was my reply.

At our next meeting, Mitch came in to meet with the team in New York. It was awkward, to say the least. Following the meeting, Mitch asked if we could meet alone. When it was just the two of us, he looked me in the eye and said, "The reason I'm here is because you failed."

I sat back, folded my arms, and thought this was going to be interesting.

He went on to say, "There are going to be changes, and you might not like them. Your new title will be director of marketing."

I told him I didn't need a title from him.

Seemingly unperturbed, he said, "Let's see how you perform over the next sixty days, and if you prove valuable, I will determine whether I keep you around and what your role will be."

Although he had retired to Mexico, he said he would be coming to New York every other week. I asked if there was anything else he wanted to tell me. When he said, "Not at this time," I got up and left the room.

To cut costs and save money, Mitch moved quickly and took swift actions, which the team nicknamed "the Purge." He wanted to get rid of overeaters—people who went to the movies more than four times per month. He decided to wage war against them. The problem with that approach was that these "overeaters" were our biggest advocates. They did all the word-of-mouth advertising for the brand. Instead of working on getting more "undereaters"—those who went to the movies two times or fewer per month—he wanted to get rid of overeaters. Mitch did a couple of things to accomplish this: He instituted capped plans. He moved customers to plans as high as $99 per month. I was informed that Mitch had the developers tweak the app to block heavy users out of the system after 2:00 p.m. each day. They would receive an error message that said ticket inventory was sold out. He even took a group of customers and just kicked them off the system and had them blacklisted so that they could not rejoin. Our social reviews were plummeting. Twitter lit up.

In my mind, this was wrong. You were taking customers' money, and if they didn't get to the theater before 2:00 p.m. each day, they were out of luck.

I approached Mitch about this, and he didn't deny it. He said that he told me that he was going to have to do things I might not like, and this was one of them. But in my opinion, this was dishonest!

I was powerless to stop it, and it went on for a few weeks. People were complaining on the Google Play store and Reddit. I was deeply concerned; not only was our reputation being ruined, I felt like we were cheating our customers. This was not the way to make money. The entire staff was upset about it. Mitch was never in the office, so I tried to manage the team's emotions. To make matters worse, when complaints started coming in through our customer service hotline, Mitch instructed the team to just turn off the phones and have customers contact us through the app. We had always prided ourselves on our customer service. The morale was sinking.

I could not pretend that I didn't know what he was doing. I contacted my personal attorney to get her advice. We agreed I had to resign if I was not going to go along with the program. First, I contacted our corporate counsel and let him know that I would be resigning and why. He was very concerned about what he was hearing and felt I needed to alert the board.

I emailed my resignation letter to Chris, who was chairman of the board at the time, laying out all the practices that had been taking place that I was uncomfortable with. He called me immediately and asked me not to resign. He said he would have a conversation with Mitch.

Moments later, my phone rang. It was Mitch. He said they didn't want me to resign, but I told him I couldn't stay with the new practices he'd instituted. Mitch assured me that he would discontinue them if I agreed to stay. He did, and I stayed.

I was trying to right the ship, but I could tell things were wearing thin between Mitch and Chris. Mitch had not proven to be the great hope he was thought to be, and money was not coming in as hoped. Chris started to claw back the equity committed to Mitch, and he drew a hard line in the sand that he was going to stop funding.

Then I heard that there was a company called Helios and Matheson (HMNY) that was interested in buying us. It was a cash/stock deal for 51 percent ownership of MoviePass. The requirements on our side of the deal would be that we would drop the subscription price to $10 per month until we reached 100,000 users. We had to reach 100,000 users in six months, and then we had to take MoviePass public. The investment amount would be $25 million.

HMNY was a publicly traded company whose main product was called RedZone. It took police crime data and put it into a heat map to let you know what parts of towns in cities you should avoid. It was getting a lot of flak from civil liberties groups like the NAACP because of the way it misrepresented areas of color and had the potential to negatively impact businesses in those areas.

HMNY's CEO was a man named Ted Farnsworth. I didn't know much about him except that he had had a string of businesses and got his big break early in his career as the owner of a psychic hotline with La Toya Jackson. We had a series of lunches and dinners with Ted, and he was very charming, but at the level we were playing at, everyone has the gift of gab and knows how to get deals done. At the end of the day, I thought the cash would make us reach an important milestone, and we still had some control in the company.

MoviePass announced the deal on August 15, 2017, and at the same time, we dropped the price to $9.95. Ted felt it was a good universal price, since Netflix was $9.95. My feeling was the price was unrealistic and not sustainable, but it would grow the user base quickly. I was learning that being a publicly traded company is completely different from being private, and if we wanted to play that game, we had to look good. We had four and a half months now to hit 100,000 customers. We sat around the office and wondered how soon we could reach that goal. Would it take four months? Ninety days? Sixty days? No one really knew.

When we opened the doors to the site with the new low price, the excitement completely overwhelmed our system. We added more than 100,000 subscribers in less than forty-eight hours. Yes, we hit our goal in two days.

In my eyes, this was fantastic. We could take the investment money, throttle back, get the model right, and continue a smart growth plan. Ted and Mitch had a completely different idea. They wanted to grow as fast as possible.

Overnight, our corporate culture changed. We were having meetings in the MoviePass downtown offices, but Mitch and Ted were meeting separately at HMNY's office in the Empire State Building. They were making all the decisions and would dictate what they wanted MoviePass to do. They even had access to the website and were changing copy and design without even discussing it with us. Ted was overstepping his bounds. HMNY didn't take 51 percent ownership until after we received all our funds, which were to come in three tranches. They had only delivered one tranche.

Since HMNY's announcement of the MoviePass deal, their stock shot up from $2 per share to $32.90. I believed the price would settle around where the public prices of the theater circuits were trading—AMC was at $12 and Cinemark at $19. Still, this gave MoviePass an overall valuation of nearly half a billion dollars based on the number of shares being traded at the $32 price point.

Over the next two months, we were growing at a quarter of a million new subs every month. The problem was that for every new subscriber, we had a negative burn of $30 per month due to their overuse. So, the consumer would give us $10 but go see four movies and cost us $30—and in New York and Los Angeles it cost us even more. This model was completely unsustainable and made no sense.

Ted and some of the number crunchers at HMNY came up with the idea that if we hit five million subscribers we would get to breakeven. They were not movie people and didn't understand this simple math that I explained to them. There are forty million frequent moviegoers in the United States. They go to the movies once a month or more. They make up 50 percent of all box office ticket sales. That group accounts for five billion dollars in revenue every year. So, if you want to reach a group of people who go to the movies less than once per month, you have to get past forty million subscribers, not five. Second, we learned from the Mather report that when those customers joined, they were going to double their moviegoing, which meant we would need to surpass eighty million subscribers to get the model to work at $10 a month, and it would cost us between $11 and $20 billion in investment capital to get there. I loudly voiced this opinion, but Ted and Mitch kept running around on news shows talking about being the fastest-growing media company in recent history.

I had less and less interaction with Mitch and Ted. It seemed like I saw them more on television than I did in the MoviePass offices. One of the last times we gathered as a company, at an off-site meeting at an ad agency in Midtown, they talked about plans and ideas for the future, but none of it was based on reality. One of the absurd ideas Ted floated in the room was that MoviePass should buy AMC Theaters. With what capital?

MoviePass continued to lose money, and we needed an influx of cash, fast. Mitch and Ted approached the MoviePass board with an offer of a $100 million credit line from Hudson Bay Capital. The structure of the deal was convoluted. It was a loan to HMNY, but MoviePass's intellectual property—the company's patents, which were under my and Hamet's names—was used as collateral. I was completely against this. We had met our threshold of performance with the HMNY deal, and we needed to slow this train down and get control over it.

I called one of my stockbroker friends and asked him about Hudson Bay. He said you do not want to do a deal with them. I went and looked up some past lawsuits, and that seemed to be the case. I brought this information to Mitch, but he said we had to keep growing and we needed the cash.

I was adamantly opposed to the deal, but the majority of the board didn't share my opinion, and thus the deal was approved.

As December approached, we were nearing one million subscribers. Mitch came to the board with an employment contract that was required for the consummation of the HMNY ownership stake to take place before the end of the year. Mitch sent around his agreement for the board's approval ahead of the meeting. It was aggressive and did not take the health of the company into consideration. The bonus compensation was based on stock price. I felt it should have been based more on the lifetime value (LTV) of customers. If the LTV is positive, you have a healthy company; if not, you have an unhealthy company. What difference does it make if you have one million customers but you're losing $30 per month on each of them?

I pushed back on several of the points in the contract, and there was not a definitive decision on the November board call.

We had a conference call with the PR teams to discuss what we would do when we hit one million subscribers. Many threw around ideas. I mentioned that Jeff Bezos had personally delivered the one millionth Amazon package to a customer in Japan. I suggested that we have Mitch deliver the one millionth Movie-Pass card personally and make a press event out of it, perhaps take the person to the movies and have a theater filled with other MoviePass members. Mitch and Ted said they would think about it. What ended up happening was after work one evening, Mitch and Ted walked down the street, stood in front of the AMC at Times Square, and took pictures of themselves holding up Movie-Pass cards looking like they were laughing all the way to the bank. That picture eventually made its way to the press. It was incredibly demoralizing for the staff to know that the image was seen by people all over the world. It wasn't the style of our brand, and it was, in my opinion, in poor taste.

At the start of the December board call, after the meeting had been called to order, Mitch said, "I would like to thank both Stacy and Hamet for all their hard work in getting MoviePass to this point, but your service will no longer be needed on the board. Your two seats will be going to HMNY."

The board at the time comprised me, Hamet, Chris, Cecelia (who worked with Chris), and Mitch.

I said, "Excuse me, why are we being kicked off the board? The board can simply be expanded to seven seats so that HMNY can be represented." Mitch said he didn't want anyone who answered to him to sit on the board. He said that he and Chris had discussed it and the decision had been made. I told him I didn't agree and hung up.

I reached out to Chris, but he didn't reply. Mitch called me, and the call between us only made things worse. I wrote a letter to the board because I wanted it to be included in the board's archives. I felt having the two founders of the company kicked off the board was a disgrace. I felt that having our ongoing participation was key to being able to save the company from this race toward oblivion. I was deeply concerned with our maintaining and protecting the current shareholder value. It was also personally upsetting to see them get rid of the only two Black members on the board, shifting to an all-white board.

Here is the letter I wrote:

December 7, 2017
To: MoviePass Board of Directors
Re: MoviePass Board of Directors Membership

Dear MoviePass Board of Directors,

During our board meeting on Tuesday, December 5th, I was asked to resign from the board. The reason given was that our CEO does not want anyone who works for the company to sit on the board.

I believe the best way to proceed is to have the board vote to remove me since I am not in agreement with this direction. The letter should reflect as much. I will honor the board's decision.

As the original founder of MoviePass, I would like to express certain views for the board to consider as it moves forward.

Diversity

MoviePass has the potential to shepherd positive changes in the movie industry, not only for the movie going experience, but in the filmmaking and the exhibition communities. It's smart business to have diverse, qualified views sitting at the decision table in an industry that is dependent on collaborative relationships.

It is also important that MoviePass have a board that embodies diversity in the seats to include minorities and women. In an industry where minority ownership in the exhibition is virtually nonexistent, while people of color disproportionately represent ticket sales, MoviePass has an opportunity to reshape views that have long created obstacles to diversity in the film industry. Additionally, recent watershed events underscore the imperative to include women on the board to ensure MoviePass is an integral part of a better and stronger industry.

Operational Presence

Having an executive from inside the company seated on the board helps to ensure a conduit of ideas between the team and CEO and board of directors. It certainly cannot hurt.

Mentorship

I've been inspired by companies that have groomed and mentored talent from within. This is something that we have been passionate about at MoviePass. Many of our valued team began as hungry interns with a passion for what MoviePass was building. They have grown into very capable executives who have contributed to MoviePass's success and bottom line. Their engagement in new technologies helps to keep MoviePass at the forefront of innovation. Consider including some of these young people in board meetings from time to time to reinforce our commitment to developing talent and allowing voices from inside the company to be heard.

Thank you for your time and for the opportunity to serve.

Sincerely,

Stacy Spikes

I am not a person who believes founders should never be removed from boards. Quite the contrary—if a founder's behavior has drawn negative attention to the company or if they have become a detriment, by all means they should be removed. But I do not believe that founders should be removed if they have different views than management or even the board itself. Those varying views are critical to the lifeblood and success of an emerging company, as well as a protective layer for shareholders. If you have no alternative points of view on a board, the company can go very quickly in the wrong direction, which is what ultimately happened to MoviePass.

If you remove founders and others reporting from inside the company in a situation where you have already received red flags about the behavior of the CEO, you prevent the board from having an honest and clear view of things that are going on that could be detrimental to the company's long-term success.

In the end, we did not prevail, and Hamet and I were removed.

FOLLOWING THE HOLIDAYS, I went back to the office to do whatever I could to try to salvage the company. On Tuesday,

January 9, I opened an email from Mitch simply stating that he wished he was in town to do this in person, but that my services were no longer needed by the company. The coward fired me via email. I shouldn't have been surprised by this, but not hearing anything from Chris was disappointing.

I made my rounds at the office to let the staff know. There was a lot of crying and disbelief. I then called Marianne to break the news. I packed up my office and walked home.

Waking up the next day and not going to work felt strange, to say the least. But I couldn't just leave everything behind me. First of all, Mitch started playing games right out of the box. He offered me two weeks' severance. Really? After I founded the company, and worked for twelve years to build that company, many of those years going without pay, you want to give me only two weeks' severance? I told my attorney to remind them I had a black binder filled with emails about some of their behavior regarding customers, and they did not want the *New York Times* to see them. We settled on something that made more sense after that. I was very glad I had been keeping those backup emails.

A few weeks later I got an email from an old friend from my music-industry days, Smokey Fontaine. He was now the editor in chief at Apple, and said that for Black History Month Apple wanted to do a feature in the App Store on the founders of Movie-Pass. It was ironic that Apple thought MoviePass's Black founders were of some importance when the MoviePass board didn't.

Apple went all out. They rented out a theater in Los Angeles, off Hollywood Boulevard, and did a full photo shoot. When the piece ran in the App store, people were shocked and excited. Black Twitter blew up. Folks were thrilled to find out that there were successful people of color in tech.

Over the next year, a crazy amount of press recognition hit. One tech article asked, "What if the Avengers were tech entrepreneurs?"

It was very tongue-in-cheek, but a fun article. Elon Musk was Iron Man, Jeff Bezos was the Incredible Hulk, Mark Zuckerberg was Spider-Man, Marissa Mayer was Black Widow, and I was the Black Panther. Pretty cool company to be in!

USA Today named me one of twenty-one influential Black professionals in tech. It was an incredible honor.

While all of this was going on, the MoviePass dumpster fire was continuing to burn. I was getting calls from the staff weekly asking me for guidance. I would try to reassure them that things would be okay, but I knew there was no way to get out of this if they didn't raise the subscription price. I stayed out of the office politics and just did my best to be there for them as a friend. But I could do the math; the MoviePass negative burn had to be in the area of about $30 million per month. And they were spending money like there was no tomorrow. Massive Sundance Film Festival party. Coachella party with a MoviePass helicopter to fly around celebrities like Dennis Rodman. MoviePass private jets to Cannes for the *Gotti* party with John Travolta and 50 Cent. Billboards all over Times Square. There were even rumors that they were going to open a MoviePass merchandise pop-up store on Sunset Boulevard in LA.

Based on what I was reading in the press, it appeared they had reinstated some of the policies that I had threatened to resign over. Customers were complaining left and right about how they were unable to use the app and unable to cancel and unable to contact anyone. In addition, even those who did manage to cancel were still being charged monthly. It was madness.

MoviePass announced they were going to get into film production, and *Gotti* was one of their first partnerships. The movie was a bomb. What was really strange was that Mitch started texting me periodically. "Hey, you should join us at the *Gotti* premiere. It would be great to see you."

Lawsuits were being filed against MoviePass, and things were looking pretty bad. The HMNY share price was falling like a lead zeppelin. Mitch and Ted were working the financial news circuits regularly, trying to prop up the falling price and build investor confidence, but it was not working. No one was buying the promise that they were going to make up the profit by using the data. What business could make $30 per month per person by selling data? The screaming customer complaints were not helping, and AMC was doing a much better job with their subscription service that they had recently launched and had a respectable 100,000 customers.

Some MoviePass customers were posting online, begging the company to raise the price. They argued that they would rather pay more and have MoviePass around and be healthy than for it to die and go away.

MoviePass reached a peak of three million subscribers by June 13, 2018. Then it began a rapid descent, almost as fast as its rise. At its height, HMNY stock traded at $32 per share on October 12, 2017; just ten months later, on August 17, 2018, the stock would fall 99.99 percent to a price of $.03 per share. HMNY had burned through over $266 million in cash.

If I, as a Black founder, had burned through that amount of investors' capital in a single year, I would have been put in jail. But these guys?

CHAPTER 15

WAKANDA

I HAVE BEEN ASKED many times what it was like to lose the company I created and watch its demise. In some ways, it was terribly hard. MoviePass was built on the work, dedication, and sacrifice of so many good people. I grieved the loss of the product of our shared passion, and for a while felt deep resentment that greed and lack of business acumen could destroy something that could have greatly benefited an industry and that consumers loved. However, I was very grateful to get as far and as high as we did. It proved that I was not crazy, and the idea had merit and resonated with the world. I also had so many proud moments on the MoviePass journey.

I remember one particular day the most. It was a Saturday, and as I often did, I decided to go to the movies in the early afternoon. The movie that I wanted to see was playing at the Regal Union Square theater at the corner of Broadway and Thirteenth Street. I love walking to that theater from my apartment because I walk up a little street called Minetta Street, which turns into Minetta Lane. This area has a significant African

American history. In the 1640s, what is present-day Greenwich Village was the first legally emancipated community of people of African descent in North America. This area was known as "Land of the Blacks" and included parts of Chinatown, Little Italy, SoHo, Greenwich Village, and Washington Square Park. Minetta Street is a remnant of a road that ran alongside Minetta Creek and connected some of the African farms in New Amsterdam. It's a beautiful, quiet street that cars rarely come down, and sometimes when I am there, I swear I can feel the sweet taste of freedom that my ancestors must have savored.

On this particular day, I walked into the lobby of the theater where there was an open room of ticketing kiosks. I checked in with the MoviePass app and then took out my card to purchase my ticket. At that moment, while I held the red card in my hand, I looked to my right and my left and saw two people who were also using their MoviePass cards. We all smiled at each other. After I got my ticket, I hung there for a moment and watched even more people check in with their MoviePass cards.

I made my way upstairs because I like to sit in the balcony. I found a seat and got settled. There was a young brother seated in the row in front of me. I saw him taking a picture of his ticket with his MoviePass app. A few moments later he looked back between the seats at me.

He said, "I'm sorry to bother you, but are you Stacy Spikes?"

I was taken aback. How did he know me? Did I know him? I told him I was Stacy, and he said, "Thank you so much for creating MoviePass. It's an amazing product. And it's so cool that a Black man created it. I mean, it kinda makes me proud."

I thanked him for his believing in us and for his kind words. They meant more to me than he knew.

―――――――

NOT HAVING MOVIEPASS as a daily part of my life, as part of my identity, made me feel a bit lost. A bit aimless. I wasn't sure what my next direction would be. I missed the team. The action. The problem solving. I missed all of it. I, like the rest of the world, got daily updates from the news about what was happening to MoviePass, but to be honest, I just didn't want to know.

Surprisingly, unlike the first time I crashed and burned with Urbanworld Films in 2000, I didn't feel completely hopeless this time around. I think seeing the evidence that the world really appreciated something I had built gave me a level of confidence that I didn't have when I was younger. This kept me afloat emotionally, and while I was sad at times, I didn't hit that level of rock bottom. But dealing with the sense of loss and failure was very real. The best way I can describe it is as if you reach the summit of Everest and then get kicked off at the top. I had failed and fallen down before, but it's a different feeling when your product has traction and recognition and then you crash and burn. Some ways it's easier, and some ways it's harder.

It wasn't a big epiphany that got me through the days and weeks after this all happened; it was something much simpler. It goes back to a saying that a friend once told me. He said, "When things are going well, chop wood and carry water. When things are going badly, chop wood and carry water." I have since discovered that the origin of this saying is rooted in Zen Buddhism. The saying actually goes:

> *Before enlightenment, chop wood and carry water.*
> *After enlightenment, chop wood and carry water.*

I took this advice to heart, and once I finally stopped feeling sorry for myself, I got back to basics. For me this meant I had to be grounded in the rituals of my daily routine. My twenty-four-hour routine looks a little like this:

Around 9:00 p.m., before I meditate prior to bedtime, I try to read something spiritually uplifting. Something I can contemplate. It could be scripture, a poem, a passage from a book—even a phrase. Then I like to visualize what the next day will look like. I like to list my actions for the day. I write this list down on a slip of paper that I carry in my pocket throughout the day. I find it helps me to stay focused and gets me out of the starting block faster. My list is usually the same every day.

✓ Wake	✓ Work
✓ Meditate	✓ Home
✓ Run	✓ Eat
✓ Walk/Feed Dogs	✓ Read
✓ Shower	✓ Plan Tomorrow
✓ Office	✓ Meditate
✓ Read Trade News	✓ Bed

This is my version of chopping wood and carrying water. I sometimes add more detail to areas of my day, and those details may vary, but the consistency of this routine is very empowering and, I believe, a key to my success and ability to accomplish my goals. I have developed this routine over time after reading many books on time management and through trial and error. I find I am more effective if I time tasks as well, blocking out and assigning times to each. Limiting the time I work on a project makes achieving goals easier. I also break up tasks using the Pomodoro Technique, which was a game changer for me. Check it out; there's lots of data and research about it.

One of the most important things I find about having a strong, consistent routine that includes exercise and meditation is that it fends off depression and negative thinking better than anything I know. When I was young and I ran into a problem at work or low cash flow, I would stop working out, eat like crap, drink diet soda, pull long hours, and sleep at my desk. I had to learn the hard way that those behaviors didn't help me. I would become a miserable human being. Now, this is not to say I don't pull all-nighters when I am on deadline for a project. I do, but the difference is I try to keep as much of my daily routine unchanged as possible. For example, I don't miss my runs—ever. No matter what. Going for a thirty-minute run when I am tired and stressed is an amazing mood enhancer. I also add short power naps into my day when I need them. Naps are so beneficial. I believe doing these things sooner would have made me a better entrepreneur, but it takes time to learn these things.

A couple of months out from MoviePass, I realized I needed an office to go to. It helps me stick to my routine. I reached out to some of the WeWork offices in the area for a single-person office and, believe it or not, my old MoviePass office was empty and available. MoviePass had moved uptown to be closer to the HMNY offices after I was gone. Being back in my old space felt comfortable and right. I went the very next day and signed a lease.

I began to ask myself, *So what is the next thing I am going to work on?* I knew I was interested in the areas of human attention and visual storytelling, from determining what types of stories people connect with to how to get traction and engagement for those stories in competitive environments. This always leads me back to my passion for visual storytelling. Visual storytelling can run from a thirty-second advertisement up to episodic series that run for multiple seasons and everything in between. And these different forms of storytelling run on three basic business models: pay-per-view, subscription, and ad supported. The challenge of them all is the fight for human attention.

I find the attention economy utterly fascinating. Companies spend billions of dollars to make sure we're paying attention to their products. And digital media has changed the game completely. On the web our attention is owned, harvested, and sold as a commodity, and we have no control over what happens to our data or what advertising we are shown.

So, my thought was, what if there was a way to allow people to monetize their own attention and be compensated for it directly and then spend it on what they wished? They would be paid for their time and attention on the web and be able at each instance to release only the data they wish to release, and their information would never sit in a central database.

I became obsessed with this idea and started to go down many rabbit holes. But I needed to figure out how much human attention is worth. I looked at NFL advertising as a start, since there was so much data there. The average football game is three hours and gets approximately fifteen million viewers. Thirty-three percent, or one hour, of the game time is just ads. The average cost of an NFL Sunday Night Football thirty-second ad spot was $783,000 for the 2021 season. This implies that the average revenue per minute for a game is $1.4 million. If we multiply that by sixty minutes, we get $88.5 million per game; divided by fifteen million views, that equals $5.90 per person. Divide that by sixty minutes and you see that human attention on that platform is being valued at $.09 per minute.

I began to ask myself, what was *my* attention worth? Would I be willing to watch ads and answer some brand's survey questions in exchange for being paid directly? The answer was yes. I have done in-person focus groups and was paid as much as $100, and have filled out online questionnaires for nothing more than finding out what my "leadership style" is. Then I ran some online polls and asked consumers if *they* would be willing to watch thirty minutes of branded content in exchange for a free movie ticket, and the overwhelming answer was yes. More than 75 percent of people polled on Google said they would.

Well, now my mental dog had a bone to chase. First, I needed to figure out how to build a product that would give consumers complete control over their data, allow them to be paid directly for their attention, and give brands better engagement with consumers in a simple and easy way. And in the process, I would introduce a new way to drive traffic to movies and allow cinemas to capture ad revenue like television in an uninterrupted way. Easy, right?

My next challenge was to figure out the use case, or the UX (user experience), as we like to call it. I was thinking it should be an app that acted sort of like a vending machine. You would go into the app and select a movie that you wanted to see. Then you would choose the format: in theaters or via video on demand (VOD). Then the app would send you one or two branded ad blocks, videos you would have to watch before you could see your movie (which is why I picked the name Pre-Show). Once you completed viewing them, the cost of your movie ticket would be covered by funds deposited in your digital wallet to use whenever you liked.

That part of the idea was simple, and I had an engineer build it out for me. I then started to take the idea around to get some counsel from colleagues I trusted. I was particularly excited to show it to one executive at a well-known electronics company. He was smart, a problem solver, and on the cutting edge of digital media. I knew he would have some good feedback for me. I went over to his office and we had a good meeting, and he asked if I would come back in a week or so to show it to his team. I said absolutely, and we put a date on the calendar.

On the day of the meeting, I loaded my prototype on my iPad and was ready to go. I sat in the conference room with my friend and three other executives, but my friend had to excuse himself to take a call, so I had to pitch these strangers on my own. I first did a PowerPoint presentation around the general concept, and they all seemed to agree with the premise. Then I moved on to the live product demo. I let them know that this was a very rough MVP (minimum value proof), a very early version of the product with the minimum requirements to make it work. I pulled out my iPad and walked them through the demo. The executive on my left asked if he could hold it himself, so I handed him my iPad.

He said, "What prevents me from pressing play and just walking away without watching the preshow?"

I sat there for a moment and then said, "Well, nothing."

He started asking me about my CPM, or cost per mille (or cost per thousand). This is a marketing term indicating the price an advertiser will pay for one thousand views of an advertisement. He said, "You will never be able to get a higher CPM rate if you can't prove people watched it, and if you can't get a higher CPM rate, people will have to watch several hours of commercials in order to pay for their movie ticket."

I didn't have a good answer for him. He was right, and I left the meeting feeling defeated. How could I guarantee advertisers that people were actually paying attention to their ads? It seemed impossible.

I went to bed that night with this question bouncing around my brain, and when I woke up the next morning, my mind had figured it out. I had been reading a lot about facial motion capture (mo-cap). It is a process of converting the movements of a person's face into a digital database. It was being used for AI and gaming engines, and the technology was impressive. What if we could use mo-cap as a way to determine whether the person was actually watching the preshow? It was something I would start to explore.

In early 2019, I got a call from my dear friend B.K. Fulton. He said he was coming to town and wanted to know if I was available to grab drinks. I said absolutely, because I always love chatting with B.K. He had been an executive at Verizon for years and was at one point interested in investing in MoviePass but was late to the round. I had met B.K. at the BFF Summit, and over the years we got to know each other pretty well. He's just one of those positive brothers you always feel great after spending some time with.

We met in the hotel he was staying at near Grand Central. He was dressed as sharply as always. We sat in two deep chairs with a black glass table between, overlooking the atrium. He asked how my family was, and I asked about his wife, Jackie. Then he jumped right into it and wanted to know what the hell was all this crazy BS in the press about MoviePass. He was referring to the constant insanity that was happening on a weekly basis. I filled him in on some of the craziest stories, and we laughed about how unbelievable it really was.

Then his demeanor changed, and he looked me in the eyes and said, "Man, I am really sorry about what happened. You and Hamet worked hard to build that company, and we were all so proud of you guys. I'm sorry, man. That just isn't right."

I got a lump in my throat, and I had to look away. I thanked him for his kind words. Then, in true B.K. fashion, he turned the mood around and said, "The real question is what are you working on now, 'cause you know they can't keep a good brother down."

I told him about my ideas around PreShow and being able to put the power of people's attention into their own hands. He loved it and, always encouraging, asked about my next steps. I said I believed there was a way to get a patent on the technology, and he asked how much it would cost to get there. I threw out a rough estimate, and without hesitation he said, "If it's all right with you, Jackie and I would like to invest."

I was speechless. The money would certainly help immensely, but I wasn't expecting this. I wasn't pitching B.K.; it was just two old friends catching up. I didn't know what to say.

B.K. leaned across the table and said, "Brother, we have to make sure you get back in that ring. You need to continue building great things. I'm sorry about what happened to you, but we are not going to let them win. We have to stick together, and if we don't come together and support you at times like this, then who will? This is Wakanda, baby, and we got ya back. Wakanda forever, brother. I will wire you the money next week; just send me the instructions."

There have been times in my life when human beings completely astounded me, and this was one of those times. True to his word, B.K. wired the funds a week later.

As things progressed, we made good advances with the technology and thought we had found a solution to the problem of verifying attention. The customer would be able to open the app, select the movie they wanted to see, and it would send them a preshow. During the playback of the preshow, if the person stopped watching or walked away, the video would pause until the person's attention resumed. The facial tracking happened only at the device level in the same way we use our face to unlock our phone. That data would not be recorded or be used in any way. It would only act in the same way a motion detector works. When someone is in the room, the lights are on. When there is no motion detected, the lights go out. We also made it possible for the consumer to be able turn off the facial detection, but they wouldn't accumulate points at the same rate since the view couldn't be verified.

When we tested it in focus groups, the numbers were amazing. Feeling strong about the product, we decided to run a Kickstarter program and allow customers to come in and try the service. On March 21, 2019, we announced PreShow to the world. Overall, the press was great. *Adweek*: "an awesome creative playground." *Business Insider*: one of "the 4 best tech innovations we saw at CinemaCon." *TechCrunch*: "Spikes has already changed how we think about paying for movie tickets, now he's pursuing a new approach." But it wasn't all great; we definitely got trolled. From *Science Alert*: "Stacy Spikes has a new startup called PreShow, and it's using a business model straight out of *A Clockwork Orange*." Not one of the negative articles mentioned that it was opt-in, meaning it was completely optional. I think we could have done a better job getting that point across.

We got fifteen hundred customers in from the Kickstarter campaign to test the product. We tested longer-format branded content that was two to five minutes in length. We showed the testers five to ten spots that would add up to about twenty minutes of ad time. Once the customer completed watching the preshow, a single-use credit card would pop up and they could go and buy a ticket to the movie of their choice. We got some really good results. Ninety percent of beta customers said they preferred the incentivized approach rather than forced ads in the middle of content. Seventy-four percent preferred longer branded content over thirty-second ads. And we had some nice quotes about the user experience as well. Two customers said, "I think this is a brilliant concept." And another said, "I'd like to watch preshows at least once a week or more."

Around this time, I was introduced to a woman who would become my partner on PreShow, Gretchen McCourt. Bernadette McCabe, who worked with me at MoviePass, introduced me to Gretchen, and we hit it off. She had worked in the movie industry for some time; she had been the head film buyer at AMC and the chief content officer at Arclight Cinemas. Gretchen was based in California and knew everyone in Hollywood. She is smart, energetic, and insightful. With the customer data from the Kickstarter, we set out to get PreShow funded. Gretchen lined up the meetings for us in LA, and I flew out and we presented our concept to each of the studios and some of the ad agencies on the West Coast.

Gretchen had seen an article in *Forbes* about this new fund called Harlem Capital. She sent the article to me, and right out of the box I loved the vision these guys had. That vision was to invest in one thousand diverse founders over the next twenty years. Standing strong and proud in the article's photo were the fund's founders: John Henry, Henri Pierre-Jacques, Brandon Bryant, and Jarrid Tingle. We reached out and made contact with them. Henri and Jarred agreed to meet with me in their office. We met in their tiny office that barely held the three of us, but I loved their hustle. They were so on point. You could feel a sense of mission in everything they said and did. During the entire meeting, I just wanted to stop, give them a hug, and tell them how proud I was of them. At the end of our meeting, I did tell them I was proud of what they were doing. By providing an opportunity for Black, brown, and female founders to raise capital, they were creating change and providing a way in for a generation of men and women who might not otherwise have had the chance to show what they could do. Leaving the meeting, they let me know that their fund only invested in post-launched cash flow–positive businesses—which PreShow was not. But they said they would discuss it and get back to me. I figured it was a no-go, but just knowing they existed filled my heart with hope for the future and all the founders of color to come.

Surprisingly, Henri got back to me and said they had

discussed PreShow in their partner meeting and were willing to lead our seed round. I was thrilled and honored that they chose to join us. B.K. Fulton was our first check for PreShow, and Harlem Capital was our first institutional investor.

The number of diverse funds is growing, and it is so exciting to see funds like Harlem Capital starting to appear on the VC landscape. I am very enthusiastic about where this is going and look forward to being part of this renaissance in any way that I can.

CHAPTER 16

PHOENIX RISING

IT WAS JANUARY 6, 2020, nearly two years to the day since I had received the email from MoviePass firing me. That morning I had another surprising email—this one a subpoena from the FBI. To be honest, I thought it was a scam or a joke, but when I received a call on my cell phone from a man claiming to be an FBI agent, I began to think that perhaps this wasn't a joke after all. The gentleman informed me that MoviePass was being investigated by the FBI and the Securities and Exchange Commission, and my presence was requested to testify on January 30. I wasn't worried that I was in trouble. I knew I didn't do anything wrong. But I had never had anything to do with the FBI, so I was a bit nervous. I contacted my attorney, who suggested I seek representation from a firm that specialized in this area, since they did not.

Over the next few days, I had several meetings with firms that specialize in dealing with publicly traded companies and the SEC. My first meeting was probably the most ridiculous. I met with a partner and an associate in their very nice, well-appointed office. The partner asked me a lot of questions and scribbled on his yellow notepad. The associate sat there and never said a word. Eventually, the partner looked at me with a frown and leaned forward. He said that this was a very serious matter and I needed strong representation, the kind of representation that only an experienced firm like his could provide. He told me situations like this could be very expensive, in the $100,000 to $200,000 range, and to get started they would need a retainer of $20,000. And then he proceeded to tell me the story of how Martha Stewart ended up in jail. This meeting felt like a scare-tactic hustle.

On the other end of the spectrum was the meeting with a partner from another firm. This lawyer didn't have a notepad, and although he asked me some questions, we talked more about kids and Christmas than about my case. He said this sounded like a low-risk situation because I was no longer working there and was gone by the time most of the crazy things happened. He suggested I just go in and have a conversation and tell them what I knew. He said if I felt I needed a lawyer, I could contact him. I trusted this guy. He was straightforward and seemed honest, and my gut told me to believe him.

On Wednesday, January 29, the day before I was to report to the US Attorney's office, it was announced that HMNY had filed for chapter 7 bankruptcy. The next day, I reported to the US Attorney's office for the East District of New York in Brooklyn, where I was questioned for two and a half hours. I told them the truth, and I knew I did nothing wrong, but as I said, the entire situation made me nervous, and I was relieved when it was over.

I fell back into my weekly routine trying to get PreShow up and on its feet. We continued to have great meetings with ad agencies, but we kept running into the same problem: everyone wanted us to have traction and an existing audience before they were willing to try the service. Plus, the gaming community was apprehensive about engaging in any form of advertising connected to their games, it felt like we were spinning our wheels.

Then Covid hit, and everything changed. We, like many companies, needed to pivot, conserve our resources, and wait out this uncertain future.

We built out some existing modifications so that we could use the preshow technology in the education space. We looked into using the technology similarly to the way the automotive industry is using technology to measure driver attention for road safety. We thought the same system could be beneficial to measure attention in the online classroom. We also focused on some easier on-ramps for the gaming sector that would allow publishers simpler testing opportunities without large commitments on their part. I was happy with what we were able to do, and despite the tough climate, we were able to raise some additional capital to keep us afloat.

In the fall of 2020, I had been contacted by a couple of different production companies who were interested in making a documentary about the MoviePass saga. I suppose the news of the HMNY bankruptcy brought MoviePass back into the press. One offer was from an independent team who said they had financing and wanted me to sign an exclusive deal with them. The other offer was from the online magazine *Business Insider*, which had a strategic partnership with CAA to bring some of their stories to life in the form of in-depth documentaries. *Business Insider* (now called *Insider*) had done what I thought were the most in-depth stories about MoviePass. They were never concerned about being first on stories but, true to their name, they did want to give the inside and most accurate version of what took place. I trusted the magazine, and more

specifically the writer Jason Guerrasio, who had written most, if
not all, of the articles on the company. Jason pitched me on the
documentary idea and asked if I would speak to the production
company. I agreed to hear what they had to say.

To be honest, I was apprehensive about the very idea of a
documentary. So often these docs and reality TV shows make
everyone look bad. My greatest concern was that for the sake of
sensationalism, my story—and the story of all the good people
involved with MoviePass—would be misconstrued and shown
in the worst possible light. Still, part of me felt that this would
be an opportunity to set the record straight about what had
happened behind the scenes to one of the most disruptive companies in the recent history of the movie industry. So many
people had no idea about the real story; they knew very little about how Hamet and I fought to bring MoviePass to life.
So, while I continued to go back and forth in my mind, I was
at least willing to have conversations with the two production
companies.

The smaller of the two was made up of two guys, one whose
father was willing to back the project. They wanted to go fast
and get into Sundance. I liked their independent spirit, but
I told them I needed to have a conversation with the second
group, and I would get back to them. I then had a call with one
of the producers on the *Insider* project. I was familiar with him
from his past positions in the movie industry, and we knew a lot
of the same people, so I felt comfortable with him. However, I
still had misgivings. He did his best to reassure me that they
would be respectful of our story, but I've been in the business
long enough to know that at the end of the day, the studio or
production company places profit and performance above all
else. I also expressed concern that every single person on the

team was a white male. I let them know that if I was going to consider going forward, we would need a person of color to be in the director's seat. They said they were open to the idea but gave a little pushback on timing and availability of directors. I told them it was a deal breaker for me.

They also wanted to have Hamet involved, but he was reluctant. He and I spoke, and his point of view was that we needed to put all of this behind us; he saw no advantage in rehashing the past. I told him that I felt strongly that history needed to be documented, and to date, no one knew our side of the story. I also thought it was important to provide the truth to all the customers, staff, and investors who lost so much. I believed they all deserved to know what had happened and what went wrong. I knew it could not bring back the money they lost, the years they gave, or the heartache they suffered, but we could at least treat them with dignity and respect and show the world we were all working to build something good and beneficial. Through these conversations with Hamet, I solidified my belief that the true story must be told. Now it was just a matter of ensuring that the project would be in the hands of a team who would honor the truth.

My experiences with the *Insider* team influenced me to decide to go with them. I agreed to give them an exclusive twelve-month option to my story. Their game plan was to bring on an unnamed production company that they were in discussions with that had a preexisting output deal. They couldn't tell me who that was at the time, but they felt that they would have a finalized agreement with this company in a matter of weeks, and my commitment in hand would help seal that deal. True to their word, in a few weeks, they gave me a call and said that the production company they were interested in bringing on board was Mark Wahlberg's company Unrealistic Ideas, which had an output deal with HBO. This was the same production team that had released the documentary *McMillion$* that had earned five Emmy nominations. I was optimistic!

The folks at Unrealistic Ideas wanted to have a conversation with me before the deal was finalized, so I had a call with partner and president Archie Gips. He expressed that he felt it was very important to tell the origin story of MoviePass, and this made me even more comfortable with the deal. I think having Unrealistic Ideas sign on also helped convince Hamet to participate. He too was nervous about how this story would be told and whether it would be handled the right way.

On February 18, 2021, the press reported that Mark Wahlberg was going to executive produce a MoviePass docuseries. I got chills when I saw all the headlines. This was actually happening!

Before there was any talk of a documentary, I had decided that I wanted to write a book about my experiences. I guess my motivation was the same as it was for agreeing to do the documentary: I wanted the truth about MoviePass to be told. I didn't have a publisher or even a literary agent, but I just started putting the story to paper. I'm not a natural writer, but I found the writing process to be very cathartic. It was difficult to relive some experiences, but the process helped me reconcile what had happened.

Since I had never written a book before, I needed some kind of structure that would give me the discipline to get it accomplished. I did some quick math and figured out if I spent one hour a day writing, within a year—maybe even sooner—I could have a finished manuscript. So, I set that as a goal for myself; I actually booked the time in my calendar, blocking out six to seven each night to just sit and write. The writing didn't always come easy. There were times I had to wrestle with the voice in my head: *Why are you doing this? Who is going to want to read a book about a guy who lost his company?* But I would just tell that voice that maybe it was right, but I was going to do it anyway. I believe that both success and failure hold lessons that might be valuable. Perhaps the stories of failure are even more important.

I also believe that anytime you decide to do something, it is important to set a goal and then complete it. It doesn't matter if it's perfect. It doesn't matter if you adhere to some arbitrary timeline. The important thing is to finish it. Accomplishment opens a world of possibilities that wouldn't otherwise be available. As the motto for the lottery goes: "You've got to be in it to win it."

When you make up your mind to do something, you will often discover that the universe will move things into place for your benefit. This is called the law of manifestation, also known as the law of attraction. You might be wondering how I can talk about God and quote the Bible in an earlier chapter and now talk about the law of attraction. My personal belief is that the two aren't mutually exclusive. The law of attraction is not a religion; it's a way of thinking. And I have observed this principle at work in my life. It doesn't always mean you get exactly what you want, but I believe you'll get what is most advantageous for you. Setting your mind to something prepares you for achievement. Success is where preparation meets opportunity. The opportunities may be around us, but too often we are not prepared to take advantage of the moment. Decide you are going to do something, move in that direction, and be ready to accomplish your dreams.

The book you hold in your hands is proof that this works. As I've said, I run daily, and for a while I would always see this one gentleman in my neighborhood. We would smile at each other and say hello, and eventually we had the opportunity to talk. I introduced myself, and he said his name was Jim Holt. At first it didn't go further than that. We would just exchange pleasantries each morning. This went on for years.

When we were all in lockdown because of Covid, I think

we both saw our daily exchange as a way to have some human interaction, so he and I started to have conversations standing six feet apart. When the inevitable "So, what do you do?" came up, I said that I was one of the cofounders of MoviePass, I had recently started another company, and I was working on a book about my experiences. He said he was an author too and asked if I had an agent. I sheepishly admitted that I didn't. Jim told me that there were quite a few authors in our neighborhood, and he offered to introduce me to a former editor at the *New York Times* who had a new book coming out.

I found out that Jim was the *New York Times* bestselling author of *Why Does the World Exist?*, and true to his word, he introduced me to Trish Hall. Trish and her husband, Larry, invited our family over for a Covid-safe dinner, also attended by Jim, his husband, and another local writer. Trish graciously offered to introduce me to her book agent, Alice Martell.

Alice lived up to my expectations of a tough, no-nonsense, extremely smart New York book agent. I loved her instantly, and she was intrigued by the concept of my book. I sent her what I had written so far, and in less than thirty days after I had told Jim I was writing a book, I had literary representation. Here was the law of manifestation at work. Had I not committed to writing a book, had I not taken action toward my goal and written a large portion of the book, I would not have been ready for this moment.

In the middle of March 2021, just a month after the Movie-Pass documentary was announced, a strange thing happened. Somebody set up a MoviePass website with a countdown clock. MoviePass had been defunct since the end of January 2020, when HMNY declared bankruptcy, and I had no idea who was behind this site. Stories ran in *Variety*, the *New York Post*, and other publications asking if MoviePass was coming back. It was eventually revealed that the website was traced to a Discord server called

MoviePass Club, which thought it would be a good hoax to boost their channel's user base. Nevertheless, the idea of MoviePass's return took hold in chat rooms on Reddit and on TikTok, with fans posting their hopes that the rumors were true.

In June 2021, word broke that the former executives of Movie-Pass had reached a settlement with the Federal Trade Commission over charges that they misled customers and failed to protect user data. (In December 2021, the former executives of Movie-Pass and its parent company would agree to pay an $8.25 million settlement to end investors' claims in New York Federal Court that they misled the public on the profitability of the company.)

In late September 2021, I received a call from someone on the documentary production team who informed me that while doing research on the project they discovered that the Movie-Pass assets had not been purchased in the bankruptcy sale of HMNY. I contacted the bankruptcy courts and confirmed that this was true. I asked the court-appointed attorney if it was still possible to make an offer to purchase MoviePass. He said I could make an offer but that the account was going to be closing in a couple of weeks, and after the files were closed it would not be possible to make the purchase. I told him that I would get back to him as soon as I could.

I could not believe it. MoviePass was available, and it could be mine again. It felt as if a long-lost beloved family member had been found. Now I just needed to find a way to bring her home. I made a few quick calls to my partner and COO, Gretchen McCourt, and to existing investors to discuss the idea of purchasing the brand back. Everyone felt it had good potential.

I was advised to use a bankruptcy attorney to go through the process, and we quickly went back to the courts and made an offer. The offer was almost half of what they were asking, but since there were no other offers they said they would consider it. We did a due diligence call to go over the assets we would be buying. Over Zoom, the trustee showed us the main files with the app code as well as the data files. But there was a problem. Most of the data files were missing. We went back and forth several times, and in the end some of the files were found and some were just lost. The trustee agreed to come down on the price since everything that was originally offered was not there. Our offer was accepted, and we moved on to the final process. We signed a binding agreement to pay the price and put the funds in escrow. Then the court had to publicly publish our bid, and there would be a twenty-one-day waiting period to see if anyone would make a counteroffer or file a complaint in an attempt to block the purchase.

The waiting game started, and I was full of nerves. My mind raced from one scenario to another. What if we didn't get it back? What if we did get it back? What if someone came in with a higher offer at the last minute? What if someone filed a complaint and blocked the deal? Around day fifteen I called the trustee to see if there had been any competitive bids. He said not yet; there had been a couple of parties who were interested earlier, but he had not heard back from them. This information didn't help my anxiety. I don't think I had a good night's sleep for twenty-one days.

Then, on November 8, 2021, after twenty-one days of waiting, an email appeared in my inbox from the bankruptcy court approving our purchase of MoviePass. It was mine once again.

That Thursday, November 11, we released a statement and confirmed that we had purchased MoviePass back. The news was covered widely by the press. It felt surreal, and the comments from the media and fans ranged from excitement to disbelief.

Now that we were getting MoviePass back, we had a lot of questions that we needed to answer quickly. Would consumers like to see MoviePass come back? Would the subscription services from the major theater chains have a negative impact on the MoviePass business? Was the brand tarnished? Would we need to modify the business model? Would the theater chains be more open to working together? How would we regain consumers' trust? The first thing we decided to do was have a listening tour with various theater circuits to see how they felt about our return. I personally emailed and called all the CEOs of the nation's largest movie theaters. We also met with the National Association of Theatre Owners and the Independent Cinema Alliance. These meetings were very helpful, and each conversation had the same question at its core: How do we drive traffic to theaters in a way that is mutually beneficial? The feedback was very insightful. All the theater owners wanted to be reassured that what happened under HMNY would not happen again. They felt that they had been burned by the previous owners and were not so willing to trust. Even though I was the original cofounder and had a long career in the industry, they still wanted to know, in detail, what I would do differently to ensure that history wouldn't repeat itself.

I assured them that MoviePass would reinstate the world-class customer service we'd had when I was CEO. MoviePass had always had high customer service ratings when I was running the company, and I vowed to bring that back. I believe customer service is one of the most important ingredients for a successful business. I promised I would always be accessible and responsive to them. I promised that we would keep them updated on progress, both good and bad. We would share data, and that, we believed, would help their businesses. I committed to treating them and the customers with dignity and respect.

My answers seemed to reassure the theater owners, and many asked how soon we could be up and running. They wanted us back by Christmas, but it was already November. I told them we hoped to be functioning by the end of summer 2022.

In addition to revitalizing our customer service division to rebuild trust in the brand, the biggest change we were looking to make was to introduce variable pricing and shift to the use of credits. In our previous version of the company, you would just pay one price, select the movie you wanted to see, and could attend a film every day if you wanted to. This was easiest for the customer, but the system had drawbacks for theaters. So we decided we would develop a new system where the customer will get a certain number of credits each month based on the subscription plan they choose. They would use those credits to go to the movie of their choice, but the number of credits needed would vary based on day of the week, the time of day, and if the theater was a partnering theater. There would be peak and off-peak shows, weekend and midweek pricing. This levels the playing field since in the old system a partnering theater and a nonpartnering theater looked the same to the customer. We wanted to allow the theater to directly compete for the customer's business.

After getting feedback from all the stakeholders—the theaters, the studios, and the customers—we felt we had a pretty good road map for the direction we wanted to take the new and improved MoviePass. We began working to build a new app, but the team agreed we also needed to find an efficient way of telling the world at large about our new vision for MoviePass. Ideally, it would be a keynote address in a movie theater; that was our brand. We set out across the city looking for the right venue, but it was more challenging than we thought. There are few theaters in New York City that have a stage. We found venues with stages but no screens. I had seen footage of a beautiful presentation at the Javits Center. I went and visited, and let's just say it was way out of our budget. Then someone asked if we had looked at the

Walter Reade Theater at Lincoln Center. I had seen movies there many times, but I couldn't remember if it had a stage. I made an appointment to see the theater, and the moment I walked in, I knew it was the place we needed to do our keynote event. They gave us two options in February. I quickly signed the agreement and put down a deposit so that we wouldn't lose the date.

As the year ended and we rolled into January, I started to doubt everything. How was I going to relaunch MoviePass? How was I going to walk onto the stage at Lincoln Center and give a live keynote address? What was I going to say? What was I thinking?

After calming myself down, I knew I just needed to focus on what I wanted to say. I wasn't presenting a new product; it wasn't ready yet. I needed to come at this from a different direction. I realized I needed to address the marketplace, the changes it had experienced since the first iteration of MoviePass, and how this new version of the company was going to benefit the industry.

During the height of the pandemic, movie theaters shut down and studios and consumers turned to streaming services. Even when the theaters reopened, attendance was down. Pundits on television and podcasts talked about the death of cinema and how the pandemic was speeding up the inevitable demise of a business that no longer mattered. I found the constant beating up of cinema annoying. I don't believe I ever heard a single person say that the pandemic was the end of sporting events or music concerts even though stadiums and music venues sat empty. The other annoying point was that cinema annually gets more attendance than all concerts, sporting events, and amusement parks combined. Cinema is the live event of the movie industry. You can watch a sports event on television, but people go to games to experience sports live. You can download music from iTunes, but there is something special about going to a venue and watching

your favorite band perform live. It's the same thing with movies. Watching a DVD or a film on a streaming service can never
compare to watching a movie in a theater with other people.

Once I locked down what my messaging would be, I got to
work putting together my presentation deck. I have several stages
to my process. First, I storyboard. I take pieces of 8½ × 11 paper
and cut them in half to produce a stack of 5½ × 8½ sheets. On
these sheets I write down all the facts and statistics, any data
points I want to include. Then I try to weave them together in a
narrative. I like to stick the sheets up on a wall and move them
around until I feel that I have the story right.

For example, if I have a statistic from the Motion Picture
Association that says more movies are attended each year than
all theme parks and sporting events combined, how do I turn
that into a story? I want the audience to know the size and power
of the movie industry and put it in context with other activities. So I would say something like, "Cinema isn't broken, it
just needs an upgrade, and we are the company to do it. Moviegoing is the number one out-of-home entertainment activity in
the United States, with over one billion theater visits every year.
Allow me to introduce you to MoviePass 2.0." From there, our
mission for the rest of the presentation is to convince the audience that what we are doing is attainable and invite them to join
us in building this new reality.

Once I know what I am going to say, I like to lay down my
background palette. I look for a theme that I want to use. What's
my color palette? Will I be using images in the background?
How will I frame the master slide? Once I have the color, the
font, the layout set, I like to grab about thirty images that I
feel will help me tell the story. The ideas from these images
come from what I have written on the sheets of paper on the
wall. I try to figure out an image that would support each fact

or piece of data. Sometimes, when the information is complex, it's easier to leave the background blank so that it does not fight the message. When I come to a stat that I want the audience to remember, I put it in bold on a slide by itself. Seventy-five percent of moviegoers want a subscription plan that allows them to attend any theaters they wish. So, I put a big 75 percent in the center of the slide.

After I have laid out all my slides, I move to my final stage of choosing effects. I use Macs, so I like to build in Keynote. I find it has the best effects, and it's easy to use. I will feature slides that transition from one to the other, have embedded videos, and graphics that load and move in a sophisticated and professional manner.

I finally finished the deck just one day before the keynote presentation. The day of our event happened to be my birthday. The HBO documentary crew was originally going to meet me at the theater but then decided they wanted to tape me going to the venue. As I stepped out of my apartment building, I saw the camera crew waiting along with our director, Muta'Ali Muhammad. This was my first time meeting him in person; we had only had Zoom calls up until now. During the negotiation process with Unrealistic Ideas I'd held firm to my condition that our director be a person of color. Muta'Ali came as a suggestion from HBO. He had done a documentary for the channel called *Yusuf Hawkins: Storm Over Brooklyn* about a black teen who was shot while surrounded by a group of Italian teens in the Bensonhurst neighborhood of Brooklyn. I felt deep confidence in Muta'Ali's ability to tell the MoviePass story.

The crew miked me up and we made our way to the subway station. Muta'Ali asked questions as we walked, and a cameraman caught it all on film. Not much makes New Yorkers take a second look, but we were noticed. A woman on the subway asked if we were making a movie. The cameraman told her they were shooting a documentary about MoviePass. The woman excitedly said, "MoviePass? I was a MoviePass member. I heard they might be coming back." At that moment, a man seated across the car said, "I was a MoviePass member too. I hope it really is coming back." That encounter really bolstered me. I was ready to make my presentation.

When we arrived at the Walter Reade, I stopped for a moment and took it all in. In a matter of hours there would be a few hundred people in this building, and I would be walking out onto the stage. The moments leading up to the event are a blur. The lights, the video, the sound had all been checked and checked again. The next thing I knew, we were about to go live. Standing backstage, I heard the music playing and the murmuring of the crowd. Someone on the crew called out, "Two minutes until go. Stand by." I moved and stood in the dark at the side of the stage. The MoviePass sizzle reel was playing on the screen, and I looked out at the crowd. I could see their eyes staring with excitement. At that moment, I wondered how a little Black boy from Houston made it to this stage at Lincoln Center. I thought of the sacrifices so many had made for this moment to be possible. If I've learned anything, I've learned this: it really doesn't matter if I succeed or fail, as long as I am willing to try. In trying, I just might make it. But more important, I can give hope to other outsiders and entrepreneurs that one day their dreams too can come true.

I took a deep breath and walked onto the stage.

ACKNOWLEDGMENTS

WRITING THIS BOOK has been an amazing journey. At times I thought I would never finish it. Like my life, I did not do any of this alone, and I want to thank some of the special people who helped along the way.

First, I would like to thank my family for their unwavering support over the years. There is absolutely no way I could have done any of this without you. Each and every one of you helped in your own unique way to keep me going on my path, especially at low points, and for that I cannot thank you enough.

Many people made this book possible. I would like to thank Jim Holt, my dear walking friend who connected me with Trish Hall, the former *New York Times* editor who introduced me to her agent, Alice Martell, who became my agent. Alice, I want to thank you for your sincere honesty and for being willing to fight for me every step of the way. And most of all, I want to thank my beloved editor, Denise Silvestro. You are absolutely amazing and give new definition to the idea of being able to finish my sentences. You made writing this book a delight.

I am so proud of the legacy we have built at Urbanworld. It is one of the most important things I have ever had the pleasure of building in my life. But hands down, if I am Urbanworld's father, Gabrielle Glore, you are its mother. It has been such an amazing journey building and nurturing Urbanworld with you. You are the ultimate combination of force and grace, so rarely found in the same person. You have the ability to move mountains and have everyone still like you at the end of that process. Yours has been the closest working relationship of my career, and most of all I love your tradition of dropping off pies at Christmas (although not having to run it off on New Year's Day). I love you, and I'm very grateful to you for being a part of our family.

In addition, I want to thank so many of the people who help to make Urbanworld the best festival in the world. There are so many of you to name, and you know who you are. I just want to say thank you for your pride and ownership over the years. I know the future of cinema is in very safe hands.

Ava DuVernay, such a large part of Urbanworld's and MoviePass's success is owed to you. You had a vision of who I and the festival could be. You were our publicist for years, and many don't know the unimaginable feats you accomplished, from getting Tom Cruise to premiere *Collateral* in Harlem or pushing me to build MoviePass and step into the limelight. Urbanworld has been your home, and you have returned over the years and continued to share your extraordinary directorial works here. Thank you, sis, for your strong hands lifting up so many, and we are grateful for all you do.

MoviePass, MoviePass, MoviePass. You wild band of movie lovers. What a journey we have been on. I want to thank all of the staff. All our early believers who hung in there with us and gave us great guidance and feedback. Our investors. And just everyone who fought alongside us in this crazy love affair with going to the movies. There's not a thing like it in the world, and there's nothing like you. We could not have built any of this without you. Special thanks to the original team. It was so much fun when we all fit in a single elevator at work and went to the movies together every Friday morning to see the new releases. Those were the days.

To my cofounder of MoviePass, Hamet Watt. You are one of the sharpest brothers I know. I have learned so much from you, and you gave me a newfound enthusiasm for always staying at the leading edge of technology. It has been a great pleasure walking with you on this adventure.

One thing in this life you need is a good lawyer. There's no way around it. The better you have, the better you will sleep. I have been represented by some of the best people, who I would call friends, and I just wanted to name some of them and let them know how much I appreciate all they've done . . . Ed and Joyce Reitler, Lisa Davis, Troy Foster, Christina Poulsen, and Barbara Courtney, the world's best patent attorney.

Community is very important, and for me the Black Filmmakers Foundation, founded by Warrington Hudlin, was critical to my career and those of so many others. Warrington would gather us every year in SoCal so that we could meet and strategize about the newest technology and make sure we all helped one another along the way. I met Gabrielle Glore and Hamet Watt at BFF. Warrington, you are a national treasure to all of us, and we are so humbled by the work you have done to make this possible. Thank you and bless you.

In the life of an entrepreneur, you need money and resources to build the ideas and dreams you have in your head. I want to thank all the investors who have ever invested in my adventures. I am humbled and grateful that you gave me a chance to build things to help change the world. I hope that I honored you.

Joey Adarkwa, thank you for being such an important part of the team and for always bringing your sense of humor when trying to meet impossible deadlines all the while being a wonderful family man.

Founders need fuel, and in the West Village we all ate at Getting Hungry. I ate there almost every day for twenty years. When you walked into Getting Hungry you were met with a huge wooden lion and lots of smiles and conversations from Joe and Hannah Dvir and Johanna Bodmer. Thank you for being a daily part of my life when I was up and when I was down.

Being an entrepreneur is not for the faint at heart. It's important to be able to step away from it all and recharge. I would like to thank my faith community, Abbey of the Genesee monastery, where I go on my silent retreats, and the US National Parks, including state park Hither Hills and campground Fish Creek Pond. I also want to express my gratitude to the Sutherland family, whom we have been camping with for years and watching our children grow up together over these summers. You showed me how to detach from my stress-driven lifework and go back to nature, which is where the real action is. Long live the Hither Highlanders!

To my wife, Marianne, and my daughter, Ellery, thank you for your love, encouragement, and support. I love you more than you will ever know.

INDEX

ABOUT THE AUTHOR

STACY SPIKES is an award-winning entrepreneur and inventor who *USA Today* named one of the twenty-one most influential Black professionals in technology. He holds several business and technical patents. He is the cofounder of the nation's first theatrical subscription service, MoviePass. In addition, Spikes is the founder of Urbanworld, the largest international festival dedicated to nurturing women and BIPOC storytellers and creators.